A HAIR'S WHISPER
From Cancer to the Courtroom

S. A. Ledlie

Copyright © 2022 S. A. Ledlie

First Edition

The author asserts the moral right under the Copyright, Designs and Patents Act 1988 to be identified as the author of this work.

All rights reserved. No part of this publication may be reproduced, stored in a retrieval system, or transmitted, in any form or by any means without the prior written consent of the author, nor be otherwise circulated in any form of binding or cover other than that in which it's published and without a similar condition being imposed on the subsequent purchaser.

DEDICATION

Samantha Keating Birtles

Contents

FOREWORD 7
INTRODUCTION 11
CHAPTER ONE 15
CHAPTER TWO 25
CHAPTER THREE 33
CHAPTER FOUR 39
CHAPTER FIVE 41
CHAPTER SIX 49
CHAPTER SEVEN 63
CHAPTER EIGHT 69
CHAPTER NINE 73
CHAPTER TEN 77
CHAPTER ELEVEN 81
CHAPTER TWELVE 95
CHAPTER THIRTEEN 101
CHAPTER FOURTEEN 111
CHAPTER FIFTEEN 117
MESSAGE FROM THE AUTHOR 119
ACKNOWLEDGEMENTS 121

FOREWORD

By David Miceli

Co-lead trial counsel, re: Taxotere MDL, Kahn v. Sanofi (case number16-17039)

"Be strong and courageous! Do not be terrified; do not be discouraged, for the Lord your God will be with you wherever you go." Joshua 1:9 (Holy Bible, New International Version, NIV)

Those that really know me know that I hold my faith very dearly, and that I will defend it and what it stands for (truth). And it has been, remains, and always will be a driving force behind what I do as a trial lawyer. In fact, it is what all trial lawyers should seek. The very product of our work – a verdict – means to speak the truth. It comes from the Latin, *verus* – true, and *dict* or *dictum* – saying. Speak the truth!

But "the truth" can be a fickle goal for some people – or some corporations – if they lose sight of what the truth actually is. Shirley Ledlie epitomizes the biblical character of Joshua in her never-ending search for the truth, and to allow the world to know the truth about Taxotere® (docetaxel). And I use Sanofi's brand name Taxotere® because when Shirley started her quest to let the world know the truth about Taxotere® there were no non-brand products due to years of patent protection (somewhat of a government sanctioned monopoly). But I digress.

Strength and courage are necessary when you become the town crier to alert the world about a risk that a drug's manufacturer insists does not exist, while its internal documents show that the company was discussing the risk more than nine years – NINE YEARS – prior to requesting a label change in the United States. These company documents contain the truth – they show Sanofi contemplating whether and how it could alert patients to an important difference in demonstrated risks: the difference between (a) the commonly accepted temporary hair loss that accompanies most, if not all, chemotherapies used to treat early-stage breast cancer, and (b) permanent chemotherapy-induced hair loss caused by Taxotere® (docetaxel).

Shirley Ledlie is that strong and courageous person that was not terrified and was never discouraged to the point of quitting her quest to get the truth out to the world. Shirley had compatriots in her quest to let the truth be known; some lost their battle with cancer still seeking to have Sanofi acknowledge the truth about Taxotere® and some lost heart and left Shirley to fight alone. But Shirley never quit, was never terrified, and when the battle came to a head in courts of law, Shirley was there to watch as lawyers for cancer survivors battled against Sanofi, one of the world's largest pharmaceutical manufacturing companies.

It is a rare exception for a trial lawyer to meet the person that first dared to challenge an international corporation over an alleged defect in its product. Often, we come to the fight after some unknown person first recognised there was a problem. We may represent persons in the second wave of pioneers to venture into battle (litigation) against a manufacturer, but to be the very first – to meet the very first to do so – is rare. But I had the pleasure to meet and get to know Shirley over the last several years. And I am proud to call her a friend. I didn't find a zealot or an ego-centric crusader. Instead, I found a humble but strong English woman who found herself living a quiet life in a small city in France and who was unlucky enough to be diagnosed with early-stage breast cancer, and even more unlucky enough to be prescribed Taxotere® without a proper warning that it may cause her to lose her hair permanently. And from that unfortunate day forward, Shirley has simply sought the truth and sought to have Sanofi recognise it as well. And, as you will read, along the way she was bullied and berated by the company seeking to conceal the truth; she has had lawyers and company physicians show up at her doctor's appointments; she had Sanofi attempt to silence her on social media and have her banned from posting. All because she wanted Sanofi to recognise and disclose the truth about Taxotere®.

And these are just some of the stories, but not spoilers by any means. In keeping with the biblical theme with which I began, Shirley tells a true David versus Goliath story. And Shirley is a worthy David in this tale. I hope you enjoy reading her story as much as I enjoyed learning it from her directly. And if you know the truth that you fight for, I urge you to "be strong and courageous; to not be terrified; and to not be discouraged."

INTRODUCTION

Since when does taking your beloved dog for its daily walkies become a cause for concern? Or feeling uneasy at the sound of footsteps or a car slowly creeping up behind you, making you twist your head around; always being on guard?

A voice in your head tells you to get a grip and stop being stupid. Then another voice whispers in your ear 'stranger things have happened', sending an icy shudder down your spine. It doesn't help matters when your elderly mother tells you to be careful each time you leave the house.

Knowing one of the largest pharmaceutical companies in the world desperately wants you to stop what you're doing feeds the irrational thoughts. They want what's on your computer and phone; any documents you might have that could help them discredit other women. They want to silence you and will go to extraordinary and shocking lengths to succeed in their mission. But have they bitten off more than they can chew with this disgruntled patient?

No doubt many of you will think this frame of mind is totally crazy. But when the truth comes out in this gripping true story, be prepared to question your 'irrational' thoughts the next time you open that innocent packet of pills or go for medical treatment.

I was diagnosed with early-stage breast cancer in

2005, undergoing surgery, chemotherapy, and radiotherapy. The following year, my oncologist informed me my chemotherapy-induced hair loss was, in fact, permanent.

He had contacted the company Sanofi, a giant in the pharmaceutical world, which makes Taxotere, one of the chemotherapy drugs I received, and they told him they were sorry it had happened to me. My once beautiful crowning glory was lost forever, replaced by a tiara of a naked scalp, several hairs, and the look of someone who's ill and still undergoing cancer treatment. I was never warned that permanent hair loss was even a possibility. I'd never heard of it before. I was devastated and was immediately plunged into a world of depression, disbelief, and suspicion.

My oncologist told me I was only the third or fourth person in the world to suffer from this adverse side effect. I needed to find those other three women. Instead, I found countless women from all parts of the globe in the same position as myself. None of them were warned about permanent hair loss through Taxotere usage either.

I then co-founded Taxotears support group with Pam, a lady from Oklahoma, and together we set out to raise awareness about this soul-destroying disfigurement and the truth behind the claims by Sanofi that this adverse side effect is very rare.

The support group was exactly that—our one safe place. Another member created a website to run alongside the group. It soon became apparent that there were potentially thousands of us with the same Taxotere signature hairstyle. Not only did we discover it was a taboo subject amongst the medical world—

perhaps because it was duped as well—but we also had to deal with brick walls at every stage and often verbal abuse from other cancer patients. We would try to explain that our problem was not that we weren't grateful to be alive, but it was the fact our oncologists did not warn us about permanent hair loss. As patients, we were denied our right to make a risk assessment and to ask for another equally effective drug which didn't carry the same risk. We were never allowed to voice our concern over the risk of permanent hair loss because we were never informed about it, and neither were our doctors.

Sanofi went out of its way to hide this hideous side effect. How can this be right? Of course, it isn't. Patients have rights. Period.

Seven years later I wrote a memoir, *Naked in the Wind: Chemo, Hair Loss and Deceit*. I thought that was the end of my journey. Little did I know it was only just the beginning of what has become a remarkable story.

CHAPTER ONE

The Aftermath

Have you ever had that feeling when you have put your heart and soul into a project that there's simply nothing left to give? You're empty. I'd had enough.

My memoir *Naked in the Wind* had been out for a couple of months and apart from checking for any sales, I wanted to put it behind me and move on. Everything I could do had been done, and if nobody else bought my book then so be it. I didn't really care. This eventful seven-year chapter in my life was over. There was much relief combined with an awareness of 'what now?' Something that had consumed my everyday thoughts had suddenly gone. Almost.

It was the right time for me to leave the support group. I'd thought about it so often, but then I'd receive an email, and I'd always end up changing my mind. The group was my baby which had now grown up and was flying the nest. It felt different this time though. I needed to tell the girls. My disfigured baldie buddies. This amazing bunch of women who had put up with my cursing and ranting over the years. These ladies, who I'd never physically met yet who knew so much about me and me them, were the only people in the world who understood how I felt.

Pam, who I'd co-founded the group with, had sadly passed away. I missed feisty Pam, my partner in crime;

she'd loved all the naughty stuff I'd get up to when trying to annoy Sanofi, and we'd enjoy our uplifting and crazy brainstorming sessions.

I drafted my goodbye email and sat on it for a week, rereading it and crying over each word. But it was the right thing to do. Send.

Weeks later, out of the blue, I received an invitation to be interviewed on a podcast called *Never Give up Hope*. How could I take part in something like this? How could I NOT? Firstly, I was surprised to be invited as my memoir had been, let's say, slightly controversial, and secondly, who'd be interested in anything I had to say?

Most of us hate the sound of our own voice, and the thought of doing the podcast filled me with anxiety. I do like to challenge myself though, and this one was definitely going to push me out of my comfort zone. Before I knew what I was doing, I accepted. I ran around the house screaming, 'Oh my God, what have I done?' My husband, John, thought it was hilarious and assured me I could do it 'no problem'.

Of course, I had to prepare myself, so after rereading my book, writing prompts on index cards, and placing them all over the office, I felt OKish. A friend who'd done several radio interviews told me to stand up when being interviewed as it makes you sound more alert and it improves your voice, something to do with the diaphragm. It made sense.

The professional intro with music strangely put me at ease instead of sending me into a tizzy. *Shirley, nobody knows this topic better than you. Stay focused.*

Carol Graham was a great host and obviously knew her subject well; she made it easy for me. In fact, it was so enjoyable, I could have carried on all night.

I woke up the next morning feeling pleased with myself. I'm just an average woman, a stay-at-home spouse, mother, and grandmother with zero experience of public speaking. I don't have a university education, but I do my best, and if I commit to something, I give it my all.

Right, that's it. I've taken part in an interview, and NOW I can move on. Wrong.

Another interview invitation arrived in my email inbox. This time it was for *Cancer Radio* with Joni Aldrich in New York City.

Now, I live in France, and my most alert time of the day is in the morning. Come late afternoon, no matter how much tea I drink, I start to wind down. Both of my invitations were from the USA, so because of the time difference, they were for the evening in France. I don't usually drink coffee unless it's mostly made with milk and with all the extra fancy bits added like sprinkles, caramel, and chocolate, but when needs must, I will force myself to have an espresso. In this case, I pushed the boat out and had a double. It was revolting, but it perked me up.

Joni was a super host, and the interview flowed perfectly. By the time I had finished, my mind was buzzing. My husband had already gone to bed, so I crept in beside him and gave him a gentle nudge to see if he was in a deep sleep because I needed to tell him all about it, and it was much more important than his sleep. He muttered, 'Tell me in the morning.' Spoil sport!

I was beginning to feel a bit like a pro. Well, not really, but because I knew my subject so thoroughly, after seven or eight years of focusing on little else, I realised I could do interviews if I pushed myself.

I honestly believed this time I was finished, that there would be no more interviews or writing requests.

Several weeks went by then unexpectedly Joni got in touch to say their equipment had malfunctioned; my interview couldn't be found, and would I be willing to do it again. *Yes of course, Joni.*

As I wrote all these prompts and looked up stats for the interviews, my old enthusiasm started to resurface. *No, stop, this isn't what I want! But what more can I do?* Surely there was nothing left to shout about. I'd given it my all, so let others take over from where I left off.

The trouble with that was that there didn't seem to be anyone willing to get on their soapbox. The support group members were probably fed up with not getting anywhere, of not being heard, and you reach a point of thinking 'why bother?' I'd reached that point more times than I could remember. Each time, I needed a break from it all then another trigger would set me off again, usually if I received an email from someone asking me for advice when they discovered their hair wasn't growing back after they had finished chemotherapy, or because someone gave them a copy of my book and they wanted to chat. On an odd occasion, I felt like screaming, 'Please, just leave me alone.' I feel so ashamed to admit that, but I am only human. In the end, each time I get these thoughts, I know I will never let these women down. Ever. There is nowhere else for them to get the answers they desperately need.

I could see a pattern starting to form, so I wasn't

that surprised when yet another podcast invitation arrived, and so it went on. And on.

Although I'd waved goodbye to the support group, their email chats still appeared in my inbox, but I restrained myself from opening them.

Occasionally, and I do mean sporadically, I would glance at the subject title, just out of curiosity, you understand. The majority were about the possibility of lawsuits, which were always one of our ambitions. I never really believed one day they would happen, but I still hoped they would. As this litigation was USA-based, it didn't interest me as I wouldn't be involved. It was nothing to do with me, but I hoped the girls would finally get their day in court. I'd already had my day in the medical claims court in Paris. As that was a total whitewash from the start, beginning with the Commission Régionale de Conciliation et d'Indemnisation (CRCI) all the way to the magistrate, I didn't hold out much hope for litigation elsewhere to come to fruition.

My latest interview was for UK Health Radio hosted by the lovely Kay Ashton MBE. Kay, or Kirsty as she is known, was delightful. She received her MBE from the Queen in the New Year honours list for Services to Children and Families. She currently works at the BBC as Creative Diversity Partner—Disability Lead. I so enjoyed our interview. UK Health Radio also has an online magazine called *The UK Health Triangle*, so a week after my interview, I authored a full-page article for them covering permanent alopecia from Taxotere and patients' rights.

Even though the support-group litigation-headed emails were increasing, and excitement seemed to be building, I still held back from reading them. Not even a crafty little peek.

A few weeks passed. One morning I was wasting time, as you do, scrolling through Facebook, when I came across a post with Taxotere in the title. It was a radio show and YouTube channel called *Ring of Fire*. The word Taxotere leapt off the page and smacked me hard in the face. Of course, I clicked to watch the video. A lawyer was being interviewed about permanent hair loss! Oh my God, this was incredible.

I was transfixed by this immaculate, amazingly articulate fast talker and his no-holds-barred interview. All the deep-seated emotions I have for Sanofi came to the fore as I watched him attack this company in a way I could not believe. My body was covered in goosebumps, and I'm sure I stopped breathing. A large screen kept flashing up pictures of the drug Taxotere as the lawyer ripped into Sanofi. Without any warning, photographs of me suddenly appeared on the screen behind him. I felt nauseous with shock.

After rewatching the video hundreds of times, I emailed the lawyer, telling him how excited I was to watch the video, that I'd loved hearing what he was saying about Sanofi and Taxotere, but also how dumbfounded I was to see my headshots being used. There were thousands of women suffering because of Taxotere; why me? He kindly replied and offered to remove the photos, but I said to leave them on if it helped as that was fine by me. Once the shock had worn off, I played the video to anyone who would watch it. The lawyer suggested he would like to interview me on Skype if they could use it for whatever they had in mind. We did it a couple of weeks later. I was pretty rubbish, sadly, so I'm not sure if it was of any use to them.

It was around this time I noticed a bulk order of my memoir had been placed. Strange. There was no way of knowing who had purchased the books; the only thing I could find out was they were bought in the USA.

Two or three days later, another bulk order, again in the USA. *Who is this mystery buyer?* I was intrigued, for sure. Unless they revealed themselves, I would never know. What with the excitement of the *Ring of Fire*'s video and my mystery buyer in the USA, my self-imposed email ban had been broken.

A couple of quiet months went by. It was nice spending time in the garden; there were always weeds to pull and vegetables to plant and nurture. Life was good. I had a little greenhouse and enjoyed hanging out in there; it was therapeutic. I call it my green meditation. An hour or two with my seedlings would help clear my scrambled brain, freeing it, enabling me to think clearly and liberating it from anything Sanofi related.

After a lovely afternoon of planting and weeding, I logged into Facebook. Well, I say logged in, but I never actually log out. I had a notification from an account I didn't recognise.

There was a beautiful young blonde lady, holding my book up. It looked as though she was at a convention for breast cancer. Behind her were posters about permanent hair loss from Taxotere/docetaxel. I couldn't believe it. On the table next to her was a row of my books. The mystery buyer had revealed herself.

I couldn't move on even if I wanted to. It was if

something were reaching out to me, letting me know it wasn't time for me to quit, not just yet.

Each time I was jolted into action, my head would feel as though it would explode, and all the old hatred for the injustice of my permanent hair loss would rear its ugly head. But even so, the old me was very much in the distant past; the maverick side to me had most definitely left the building. It certainly wasn't the last thing I'd think about when climbing into bed each night, like in the days of old.

Later I received a private Facebook message from an advertising company representing lawyers. They had bought my book initially and, after reading it, ordered more copies to give to all the staff and lawyers, and the second order was to take to this convention. That solved the puzzle.

Sales of my book increased. There was a sense of excitement in the air as though litigation in the USA was actually going to happen. *Please, please, please let these women get justice. Somebody needs to force Sanofi to take responsibility for its inhumane actions against women.*

The usual pattern followed: Inactivity. Peace. I stopped reading the subject titles in the emails from the support group, again.

I would still be contacted by desperate women, looking for answers, searching for help. I put them in touch with the support group to hopefully find what I couldn't provide anymore.

Months passed. Autumn arrived. We live just outside Toulouse and are blessed with lots of sunshine and beautiful autumns. The leaves on the trees were just starting to turn into their rainbow of warm colours.

The long sizzling summer was on its way out, and the dip in temperature during September and October was a relief. We say the same thing each year then by the end of November we want summer back. There's no pleasing us, eh?

Soon, spring 2018 was just around the corner. I'd spent the last two months planning what vegetables and flowers I would grow. If you're a gardener, you will get the excitement of the outlining, working out what to grow where and looking through the seed catalogues.

Even though I was engrossed in all things green, I couldn't shake off an eerie feeling something big was heading my way. My unexpected appearance on *Ring of Fire* had unnerved me. Had I known what was waiting for me just around the corner, I might have packed a bag and left town.

CHAPTER TWO
Litigation

March arrived and with it an email from an American lawyer from the Taxotere litigation group. My years of raising awareness in my own, let's just say, unique, way had not gone unnoticed. We chatted and of course I eagerly agreed to help. I certainly didn't need any encouragement.

I started putting together all my paperwork and printed out hundreds of emails I'd accumulated from doctors, specialists in hair loss or scalp cooling, and oncologists, not to mention my own medical team. I also have letters and emails from Sanofi, some admitting they knew permanent hair loss could happen and others telling me not to contact them again. Like that was ever going to happen. Everything went into a big file.

It was such a privilege to meet up with this amazing group of lawyers to hand everything over and signed a protection order. The mountain of paperwork, emails, and studies I've printed out over the past sixteen years since discovering that my hair loss was permanent would give Mount Everest a run for its money. Much to my husband's despair, it can be found in piles all around the house. Disorganisation is my middle name. My inbox account is crammed with thousands of emails, many left unread. I'll get round to them one day.

It was around this time I discovered a website called DocketBird, which I can only describe as an electronic court filing system. Occasionally the files can be opened by the general public, but some can't. If you really want to read one that won't open, you can pay three of four dollars for the pleasure. DocketBird was my new best friend. An automated system sent me a notification whenever a new court document was filed; I could to see the title which gave me a clue what it was about. This was useful. If I saw a document of real interest, I bought it.

One day I received one of these notifications and saw my name in the subject title. Of course, I handed over my dollars without a second thought.

It was a pivotal moment. Reading this court document about something I had done many years ago was a shock in itself, but to see in black and white Sanofi's behind-the-scenes reaction nearly caused me to self-combust. It immediately took me back to the night in question, eight years previously, when I'd gone on a Facebook rampage after finding the page for Sanofi, which they'd oddly named Voices, and I saw they were asking for suggestions they could use for a new logo.

The temptation was too great for the then naughty me to ignore, and I ended up posting photographs of my scalp so many times—I've forgotten how many—with an explanation about how their drug Taxotere had caused my permanent alopecia. It went viral and caused such a furore that not only did Sanofi remove all my posts, just for me to post them again, it eventually ended up bringing their page down completely for a few days. Of course, pharma groups and bloggers had a field day and were using my post as an example of what pharma companies shouldn't do when faced with a disgruntled patient. In other words, Sanofi's handling of this drama was an embarrassing social media faux pas. In fact, this episode has since been included in various books and articles on what *not* to do.

Sanofi ended up putting their new-style Facebook page back up and blocking me from being able to post.

Anyway, this pivotal moment came from that very Facebook incident. I downloaded the DocketBird document and couldn't believe what I read.

"In response to the article and the posts, Sanofi's communications department formed a Rapid Response Team. (Ex. B, Malia Dep. 298:6-302:7.) Part of the Rapid Response Team's responsibility included monitoring the Voices page on Facebook twenty-four hours a day to remove any posts about Taxotere and permanent hair loss. Sanofi shortly thereafter hired an outside company, InTouch Solutions, to conduct this around-the-clock monitoring of its Facebook page. At Sanofi's direction, InTouch logged and removed posts about permanent hair loss, blocked the user posting about it, and reported the user to Facebook to have her banned from the platform."

Oh. My. God. A Rapid Response Team to deal with me posting the truth about possibly one of Sanofi's best-selling chemotherapy drugs. What does that tell you? I'm surprised the company didn't send a SWAT team out to pay me a visit then they wouldn't have had to bother hiring InTouch Solutions to monitor my postings. Well, I hope they charged Sanofi an absolute fortune for the pleasure.

The court document continued.

"But the user was undeterred, posting that same post twenty-eight more times after it was removed. And twenty-eight more times, InTouch Solutions – at Sanofi's direction – scrubbed the post from Facebook."

Twenty-eight times? You can't say I'm not determined. Mind you, had I known they'd formed a Rapid Response Team, I might not have gone to all that trouble. All they had to do was reach out to me, but no, they would rather spend God knows how many dollars trying to silence me instead. That says more about them than it does me. Maybe they should have thought of a more appropriate page name than Voices. Maybe Silence. Sanofi sure as hell didn't want to hear my voice.

I read this document umpteen times, not believing what it was telling me; they had tried to get me banned from Facebook. How dare they! I was livid. I wasn't going to forget this in a hurry. It was impossible to get my head around the fact they'd hired a company to silence me and other women on social media. InTouch Solutions went on to use this 'silencing of an angry patient' for their company's promotion. I hope they feel proud of themselves. Surely it shows them to be unscrupulous and void of any moral compass, and it's certainly nothing to be proud of. They didn't shut me up, so I'm not quite sure what they were so proud of.

For days after, I was glued to DocketBird for any more scandalous revelations that might appear. And yes, there were more. It was the most bizarre feeling to see my name in print on court documents in a foreign country. Surreal and a little unsettling. I was starting to have concerns about what, if any, the consequences would be for me. My mind was racing. I knew my name was down as being a possible witness, and I had absolutely no problem with that. But at the same time, I knew that with all the crazy online conversations with the support group over the years I doubted I'd sound very credible. So many of these 'conversations' and 'rants' took place when I was at my darkest place, full of rage and frustration, but nonetheless any defence team would have a field day with it. At that point in time, I didn't think there was anything left I could help them with. They'd had everything from me.

It seemed as though every time I looked at the latest court document filed, it had my name attached. One side was arguing that my information was relevant to the case, and the other was saying the opposite. Of course, if it came out in court to a jury that Sanofi had hired a company to silence a cancer patient, and how much time and money they'd spent trying to implement this immoral act of censorship, I doubt any jury would look favourably at that. So, it was no wonder Sanofi didn't want that episode coming out. In the end, the judge decided against having anything with my name, or anything I'd done while raising awareness about Taxotere, from being mentioned at a trial. Not even an acknowledgement that a support group existed. Just what Sanofi wanted: we, the thousands of breast cancer patients, sufferers of permanent chemotherapy-induced alopecia (PCIA), didn't exist. I'd love to know how the court came to that decision when it's so very relevant in the Sanofi shameful cover-up. We were relevant enough to garner so much attention from Sanofi when the company was trying to silence our voices—to borrow Sanofi's terminology—but when it came time to tell the story of Taxotere in front of a jury, Sanofi wanted to silence our existence again. Unfortunately, the court agreed with the company. Sad.

The evening of July 10th, 2018, was one for celebrating. The final whistle blew in the World Cup semi-final, putting France into the final after beating Belgium 1–0. Within seconds, our streets were full of cars flying their beloved tricolour flags and hooting their horns. I was sitting on the terrace in the sweltering heat to soak up a little of the electrifying atmosphere when my mobile rang. It was one of the lawyers that I had given my paperwork to.

He had a message for me from Judge North who was overseeing the litigation.

Would I be willing to save Sanofi time, effort, and, of course, money and give everything I had to the Sanofi lawyers to spare them from trying to issue me with a subpoena to take my deposition as a foreign national living in France? In all honesty, did anyone really think I was going to do Sanofi a favour? It was laughable. Did Judge North, knowing what he knew about me and what I'd done, really think I would help Sanofi out? I can't believe for one minute any of them thought that was ever going to happen.

My reply was simply, 'Tell Judge North that Sanofi can go take a hike.' If they wanted me, they could go through all the appropriate channels available to them. I would rather go to prison than voluntarily help them. I will never forget that Sanofi hired InTouch Solutions to silence me. Ever.

I wondered if they would bother with a deposition. I had no idea how Sanofi's lawyers would go about it, but I did discover that France does not recognise depositions. Would Sanofi really go to all the trouble? Surely, I wasn't of *that* much interest to them as I've continued to be an open book for as long as I can remember. *What have I got, or what do they think I have, and what do they want to do with it?*

Knowing Sanofi as well as I do, and understanding their ambition is to silence me, disband the support group and anything else connected to us, they would pursue it to the end, no matter how much it cost them financially. In my mind, and based on my experience with them, there are no depths to which this company will not stoop. And I have learnt quickly that the lawyers Sanofi retained to defend the company would live up to Sanofi's model.

The company's Achilles' heel, though, was the trail of strong, determined, disfigured women that it continued to underestimate.

CHAPTER THREE

Infiltration

The support group's admin had always been hot on vetting anyone who wanted to join. We'd all assumed Sanofi would try extremely hard to gain access to our private and intimate chats. The group had functioned perfectly over the years using the Google Groups email system.

An unwanted email arrived in my inbox. It was from Google's legal investigations support. Oh no! What NOW? Everything was starting to gather pace.

'SUBPOENA TO PRODUCE DOCUMENTS, INFORMATION, OR OBJECTS OR TO PERMIT INSPECTION OF PREMISES IN A CIVIL ACTION To: Google LLC c10 Corporation Service Company 2710 Gateway Oaks Drive, Suite 150N Sacramento, CA 95833

YOU ARE COMMANDED to produce at the time, date, and place set forth below the following documents, electronically stored information, or objects, and to permit inspection, copying, testing, or sampling of the material: Alt [sic] non-content information from the Google Group called "Taxotears," including but not limited to all documents and electronically stored information regarding the following: • All former and current "Taxotears" users' ~ names, IP addresses, usernames, e-mail addresses, and any other contact record details; • Ail [sic] former and current "Taxotears" users' dates of membership; • Access logs of all former and current "Taxotears" users; • Information sufficient to show the recipients, senders, dates sent, dates received, dates read, and dates deleted of "Taxotears" e-mails, e-mail attachments, or other posts or messages sent or received within, from, or to the "Taxotears" Google Group; • The "Taxotears" Google Group settings, both current and legacy; • The current number of users and legacy user counts of the "Taxotears" Google Group; and • The current number of posts and legacy posts available to the "Taxotears" Google Group, including the number of posts and legacy posts by each former and current "Taxotears" user. The term "users" as stated throughout this subpoena includes all "Taxotears" administrators, owners, managers, members, and custom roles, as well as any other current or legacy Google Groups roles.'

It was signed by the law firm Shook, Hardy and Bacon. I felt sick. The subpoena went on.

'YOU ARE COMMANDED to permit entry onto the designated premises, land, or other property possessed or controlled by you at the time, date, and location set forth below, so that the requesting party may inspect, measure, survey, photograph, test, or sample the property or any designated object or operation on it.

The following provisions of Fed. R. Civ. P. 45 are attached. Rule 45(c), relating to the place of compliance; Rule 45(d), relating to your protection as a person subject to a subpoena; and Rule 45(e) and (g), relating to your duty to respond to this subpoena and the potential consequences of not doing so.'

Shook, Hardy and Bacon weren't content with the thousands of our private emails already gained from the support group members involved in the litigation; they wanted to destroy us. Sanofi wanted us gone, disbanded. It was also obvious they would use any joke or light-hearted conversation we'd had in the support group to ask the jury how could these people possibly be depressed when we were laughing or telling jokes. Isn't that how defence lawyers work? We've all seen the movies. The fact that Sanofi rendered me, and others like me, disfigured and naked in the wind does not mean that we have never laughed again. On the contrary, we move on with our lives as best we can, but we are always bald. Forever bald, and all because a company chose not to inform cancer patients about a risk it knew about.

This subpoena sounded the death knell for our support group, the one sacred place where we all spent time together, helping each other. It was our one safe place. We were being violated and victimised by Sanofi yet again. This legal action against Google, giving Sanofi access to OUR group, was rendering it not fit for the purpose that it was created. How could it be right for a law firm to gain access to our private health information, our contacts, and our thoughts? It stank.

I felt so sad that it had finally come to this. So many members were not part of the litigation and didn't even live in the United States, so this seemed grossly unfair. Google added that we could send a file-stamped copy of a motion to quash or other type of formal objection by a certain time and date. But really, what was the point? Besides, I would have to pay a lawyer to draft a motion. I would have to let Sanofi and its lawyers have what they wanted, but I would also hope someone would take action to prevent or limit Sanofi's intrusion. I knew our spirit would never break, but it was always one blow after another. As for me and others like me, we found Sanofi to be a spiteful and bitter company, willing to grind into submission anyone who dares question its product. But hell hath no fury like a woman wronged, and we do not submit.

We now knew for sure that the enemy was reading every single message between us. I couldn't help but cringe at all the profanatory tirades in many of my earlier emails. I know that one or two of the girls hated my crazy outbursts, but I struggled with the frustration of not being heard, shouting into the abyss and the enablers allowing Sanofi to be a law unto itself. Oh well, I could do nothing about it, so why bother worrying? I suppose my occasional tirades painted a picture of someone who was unhinged, but at least you couldn't say I wasn't enthusiastic. And colourful. Very colourful!

My thoughts kept turning to Pam, who I'd co-founded the group with. She would have been so excited about having her day in court. She deserved it, that's for sure. Sadly, it wasn't to be, but I liked to think she was looking down on all this, sticking her middle finger up at Sanofi and giving a strong, arm of strength salute to all the women who were going to be filing lawsuits.

In a way, it was disappointing the same legal action wasn't being conducted in France. I wouldn't have the stamina or inclination to go through with it, but I would like to see it happen for the women in France who have also been lied to, disfigured, and denied their patients' rights.

The years of speculation over possible legal action were now materialising before our very eyes. It was still hard to believe. Some of the girls had contacted law firms over the years, and nobody wanted to touch this one with a barge pole. I don't suppose they had the stomach or financial pot to weather the fight. To go up against one of the largest pharmaceutical companies in the world, you would need nerves of steel and an expense account to match theirs.

Sanofi's access to our group's messages wasn't without one positive, though. It meant that any message we WANTED them to read would reach its intended mark. It would hit the right spot. But that is behind us now, and Sanofi still maintains its indignant position of entire disinterest in the women it has disfigured. Business as usual for Sanofi, I suppose.

CHAPTER FOUR
Resurfacing

As I reached forwards to grab the outer strand of the web, a spider scuttled towards me, dragging me back from freedom: I *think* I want to break free…

I could no longer fight against the call for duty. But this time was going to be different: I wanted to raise awareness in a controlled manner. I'd learnt so much over the years and was certainly no longer this volatile, crazy, screaming banshee. Instead, I was restrained, more composed and would now always hesitate before replying or Tweeting.

My name continued to be splashed about on DocketBird with the words subpoena and deposition in the same discussions between both sets of lawyers and the judge. I imagined by now Judge North must be sick to death of hearing my name, especially as I didn't see I was relevant to any of it. But the discussions continued, and I carried on monitoring. It would have been great to have my own InTouch Solutions to do my dirty work for me during this time.

Eventually Shook, Hardy and Bacon decided they were going to apply to subpoena me and fly over to France to take my deposition. This was not going to be an unchallenged ride for them. I wondered if the French courts would even allow it. The process involved them making an application to the court in

The Hague. I believe Judge North had to OK it first from what I can gather. So much trouble and expense, and for what? Did they just want to intimidate me? Try to shut me down permanently? Surely, they knew by now that wasn't going to happen. They had already rendered the support group system useless, but there was still the group's website. They were chipping away at us bit by bit, and no doubt the website was high on that list. I think they'd probably underestimated us, our strength, and the unwavering determination we had. With our group, Sanofi hardly behaves like the company it claims to be: 'chasing the miracles of science to improve people's lives.' (reference: www.sanofi.com/en/about-us/our-purpose)

One of the ladies from our group had written a blog. I had no idea of the content, but I read Sanofi was taking her to court for it, even though she had taken it down not long after posting. This type of action would have the oppositive effect of the intention behind it. Has Sanofi never heard the line from the Helen Reddy song 'I Am Woman'? The company was acting like the playground bully. So apart from living with permanent hair loss and posting a blog in anger, she was ordered to pay Sanofi.

The number of women filing lawsuits was climbing every day. Women who had questioned their medical teams or gone onto the internet and forums, looking for answers, were discovering the true culprit of why they will look like cancer patients for the rest of their lives. They were certainly interesting times, especially for the bystander.

CHAPTER FIVE
You've Been Served

I had a sense of foreboding with the subpoena hanging over my head. I might forget for a day or two then it would hit me again. The worst bit was not knowing if it would be allowed, and if so, when would I be contacted? Would someone let me know if it were denied, or would I read it on DocketBird?

It would send a shiver down my spine when I thought about how brutal Sanofi had been and continued to be. Maybe the company hates me as much as I hate them. The only difference is Sanofi has the money to do whatever they want, and I don't. What depths would they stoop to? The answer to that must be 'unmeasurable'.

Would a speeding car plough me down as I was walking the dog one day? I started to change the times I took Mum's little dog out. When I left the house, I would instruct my mum not to answer the door if anyone rang the bell, no matter who they said they were, and to keep the doors locked, always

Months went by. Just when I'd almost forgotten about it, a registered letter arrived. There it was in black and white telling me I had to attend the *Tribunal de Grande Instance de Toulouse*. Yikes! Triple yikes! It was really happening.

From what I could gather, the application went from

the court at The Hague then to a court in Paris, who OK'd it, then down to the court in Toulouse where it was given the final go-ahead.

What a lot of trouble and cost. *What is wrong with this company?*

Of course, the subpoena was in French, and French legal jargon isn't my forte, but I could work out the gist of it, especially the extensive list of what I had to take with me to hand over on the day. I was being forced into giving things to Sanofi's lawyers so they could possibly use them against the very women I'd worked so tirelessly to help over many years. It felt as though I was being assaulted by the same company that had physically and mentally assaulted me years ago, leaving me a woman stripped of her hair. How dare Sanofi attempt to FORCE me to give its lawyers my personal emails, documents, or anything else? This was my property, and I wanted only to give it to who I chose. The subpoena requested a copy of:

- Social media publications
- Discussions on forums, groups, and blogs about Taxotere hair loss
- Emails from the support group
- My correspondence with Dr Bourgeois (oncologist in Le Mans) and Dr Miguel Martin (oncologist and Head of Medical Oncology Service (Hospital General Universitario Gregorio Marañón, Madrid, Spain)) from 2008 onwards
- Medical documents from 2009 onwards
- Any other documents I had about Taxotere causing hair loss from 2006 onwards

At the bottom of the page, it said if I failed to turn up without a valid reason, I would be fined 10,000 euros. In that case, I'd better go.

The feeling of betrayal overwhelmed me, cutting to the core. The group members' chats were private and personal. We would talk about all sorts of medical conditions and subjects, including our vaginas. Throughout the years, I'd built relationships with various doctors and experts, and I'd be damned if I was just going to hand these emails over to Shook, Hardy and flippin' Bacon without a fight. Some of the girls had talked about their sex lives too, so I had no intention of handing the messages over unless it came down to being forced to give them or pay a fine. I had to think of a way out.

One beautiful, sunny morning in May, I took a long drive over to the other side of Toulouse to have coffee and a chat with my friend Stella. Now, Stella is not only beautiful and intelligent, but she's also a retired criminal barrister. I needed to talk to someone who would understand what I was facing. Over frothy, caffeine-laden coffees, I explained how stressed I was about the thought of being interrogated by people who weren't exactly fans of mine, getting all this paperwork together, and how I was going to find everything I'd ever posted on social media. Gathering thirteen years of loud, opinionated commenting was going to be an impossible task as I had no idea where I'd posted most of my thoughts. Then I poured my heart out about the treachery I felt having to hand over the support group conversations, especially the vagina and sex-life ones.

She was astonished at how it could be allowed over here in France because of the strict General Data

Protection Regulation (GDPR) and wondered if I would possibly be opening myself up to potential litigation from any of these women. It was something I knew nothing about, one of those things I'd heard of but hadn't paid any attention to. We had a lovely morning together, and she filled me with the confidence that I could handle this.

It was a happy drive home, and as I stepped through our front door, I felt a different person to when I'd left earlier that day.

The first thing I had to do was Google the GDPR. There were so many categories, but I started to work my way through them one by one. Then I found exactly what I was looking for, one that covered personal information concerning health and medical treatment. I vaguely remembered one of the members' emails containing her mother's health and other personal issues. This category seemed the perfect fit.

I knew exactly what Sanofi's lawyers would do with these emails. Each and every word would be scrutinised in the hope of finding a comment or an experience that had happened to the individual even forty years ago that could be used against them, to plant a seed of doubt in a juror's mind, or even to get the person kicked out of the litigation.

Of course, they were doing their job, but it felt like a never-ending witch hunt. Sanofi wanted to purge the world of 'Taxotears', and that was never going to happen. Not if we could help it. We were going nowhere.

Rereading a particular section of the GDPR over and over convinced me that it was the right avenue to go down. Surely Shook, Hardy and Bacon would know this existed? Perhaps they didn't work internationally? I thought I'd read on their website they did, or it could be they just thought I'd roll over and comply to their intimidating demands.

I called Stella and told her what I'd found and that I believed it to be the correct category. She offered to help put something together for me. At the time her daughter, Teddy, was a budding law student, and Stella was going to ask her to help too. It's times like this that make you realise there are kind people and amazing friends who will go out of their way to help you fight for justice.

I had to be at the court in the Toulouse city centre at 9 a.m. I live thirty minutes away, and the morning traffic is bumper to bumper. I had zero intention of getting up at 5 a.m. to face a day of interrogation by the defence lawyers, so a hotel room for the night before was necessary. I would also need parking, and I certainly wasn't going to pay for any of it.

From what I could gather, whoever instigates a deposition is liable for the expenses, but this was for the USA. I then found the *code de procédure civile française art. 748* which is more or less the same thing for here in France. I wrote that article number down on a scrap of paper to keep stuffed in a pocket on the day concerned.

I had no idea where the court building was, so after locating it on a map, I found the nearest hotel and booked a room for the night before. I decided to park my car at a large shopping mall on the outskirts of Toulouse and get an Uber to the hotel. That was it, all sorted.

It took me the best part of two weeks downloading

everything they were demanding from me, but finding all the blogs, articles, and comments of cancer forums that I couldn't even remember the names of was painstakingly arduous. For someone who is a scatterbrain and totally disorganised, it was hell. All I could do was my best.

I printed out emails I thought the Shook, Hardy and Bacon lawyers were already in possession of, so I had at least a bit of paperwork to hand over even though it was useless to them. I put everything else on a memory stick, hoping I wouldn't be forced to give it to my nemesis.

I thought it might be a clever idea to contact the support group and ask the girls if they would give me permission to provide Sanofi with all the thousands of emails I had. If I couldn't get them all to agree, it would be helpful ammunition to present to the judge. I got replies saying, 'Yes, I'm past caring,' and others that said adamantly, 'Absolutely not.' One member said 'yes', I had her permission, only for her to change her mind days later. I loved that she changed her mind.

As the date got nearer, I became increasingly nervous. Fear of the unknown, I suppose. Just what *was* a deposition? I had no idea, so I had a look on YouTube. Everything I could find had taken place in the USA. I came across a training session for lawyers on how to take a good deposition. *That'll do*! After watching it a couple of times, I felt it gave me insight on how the lawyers might tackle me, and I also understood how they can use techniques to trick you into giving away more than you should. The key message seemed to be only to answer the question asked in the shortest way possible and only if it was an actual question. Sometimes they might make a statement that sounded like a question, but in fact wasn't. *Okay, I've got this. I can do it.*

The afternoon before D-day, I packed an overnight bag and threw in my memoir *Naked in the Wind*, thinking I could flick through it to try and refresh my mind from thirteen years ago.

Checking in at the hotel made it all real. This was happening, another bizarre episode to this whole saga that began in 2005. Little did I know when I was first diagnosed with breast cancer, the journey I was about to start: all the twists and turns and all the appalling treatment from Sanofi; even after thirteen years, the company was still trying to bully me. Oh well, let their lawyers do their best. David and Goliath; multi-billion dollar/euro company vs me.

My hotel room was nice. On one side I had a view of the Garonne River, and the windows that formed the corner looked across the road towards the courthouse. I hung up my clothes for the following day, threw my book on the bed, and put my sandwiches in the fridge for later. I just wanted a relaxing evening without having to go out and find somewhere to eat. I don't like dining alone; it makes me feel too self-conscious. I FaceTimed a lifelong friend who had gone through it all with me, every step of the way from the beginning. As it happens, she has also suffered from PCIA but to a lesser degree.

The hotel provided the usual collection of bathroom products, so I ran a bubble bath. The all-windowed bathroom was situated in the corner of the room, so I hoped that the tinted glass was preventing me from providing a naked public show to the street below.

I sprawled out on the bed in my nice fluffy bathrobe, unwrapped my sandwich, and turned on the TV, only to switch it off minutes later. It was impossible to stay focused, so I grabbed my book and flicked through the pages, trying to jog my memory of the important dates or at least a rough timeline of it all. I prayed I wouldn't make a total idiot of myself the following day. At this point I didn't know if the deposition would be video recorded; it had previously been mentioned on DocketBird that it had been requested, but the final say was down to the French judge.

CHAPTER SIX

Deposition Day

My alarm clock buzzed into life. I hit the snooze button. *Another five minutes, that's all I need.* It only seemed like seconds before it came on again. *Oh my God, it's D-day*! My heart pounded as I clambered out of bed and jumped in the shower. It was so weird being in the shower and looking down at the street.

I wanted an early start so I could go into the restaurant for breakfast before it got busy. Luckily, only two tables were occupied, so after grabbing orange juice, yogurt, and fruit, I chose a table and called my husband, John. I took my time eating breakfast as it was less than a five-minute walk to the court. Back in the room, I put make-up on and packed my bag. This was surreal.

My constant glances at the time only made it go slower. How dare Sanofi put me through this after everything else? My dear old mum refers to Sanofi as 'those bastards' but I think 'mother f******' is more appropriate.

This was it. *I am woman, bring it on*.

After checking out of the hotel and glancing up at the bathroom windows, I only had to walk a short distance to join the long security queue to enter the courthouse.

They searched through my overnight bag, and I wondered if they'd ever had a bag before with PJs in. After searching the vast entrance with its old-fashioned signposts for different courtrooms, I decided to ask at reception because I couldn't see anything even close to my courtroom number. Once I'd presented my invitation (for want of a better word), reception staff directed me to a small table with a couple of people standing behind it.

As soon as I showed one of the ladies my paper, her face lit up.

'Oh, good morning, Madame Ledlie, we have been expecting you, and I'm here to escort you to the courtroom. Please follow me,' the young lady said with a huge smile. We strode across the huge marble floor and entered a lift using her security card.

'We are very excited because it's not every day we have American lawyers coming here.' She could hardly contain her excitement. Our journey continued down long corridors, again using her security badge to enter yet another labyrinth. It took an age to reach a reception area where she told me to take a seat.

The door opposite me was half open, and I could see a few people walking around, then I noticed the plaque outside which had our courtroom's number on. People entered and left, and I sat there trying to keep my nerves in check. I swear my breakfast of mostly fruit was starting to ferment. *I'm going to wake up any minute now.*

Another door opened, and in walked the very welcome, familiar face of Karen Menzies, the plaintiff's counsel, who I'd previously met and given paperwork to. She had come over from the USA, and she was accompanied by her French lawyer from Paris, wearing his black robe and an epitoge, a long black scarf with a white rabbit-fur (I think) end. *Oh boy, this looks formal.*

They walked straight into the room, and moments later, two lawyers representing Sanofi walked in with their female French lawyer, also in formal attire. The door closed, leaving me sitting there to listen to their muffled voices and my breakfast rumblings, and to ponder what lay in store for me. I had a feeling it was going to be an uncomfortably long day.

My mind strayed to the objection I was going to throw into the works to hopefully scupper Sanofi's plans. *Can I really go through with it, or will I chicken out at the last minute and just hand over the memory stick? I've got to keep my nerve; I can do this.*

The judge and the court's clerk entered the reception area, walking straight over to me to introduce themselves, making me feel very at ease and welcome. I wondered what the judge thought about the day's deposition involving American lawyers, a British woman, and a French company. Would there be any repercussions for me when, no doubt, lawyers for the defence brought up certain indiscretions of mine from years ago?

Eventually someone called me into the room. About twelve people sat around a huge table, all staring at me. *Oh my God, so many people!*

I'd already planned not to wear a wig as I only use them occasionally due to the unbearable itching, mobility, and the heat they generate, especially in the summer when our temperatures soar. However, I never leave the house without a hat or turban.

Looking over to my right, I spotted a coat rail and a table where my bags could be kept. This was the moment of truth. Placing my bags down, I then removed my coat, making sure I took my time putting it on a hanger, trying to compose myself. Then reaching up to my head, I took off my hat. So far, so good. *Now I have to turn around.*

A sea of embarrassed faces greeted me. You could have heard a pin drop. *Yes, folks, THIS is why I can't go outside without covering up this devil's hairstyle. Suck it up, Sanofi lawyers, because it's what you'll be looking at all day while you interrogate and bully me when I've done nothing wrong.*

I don't think the court's staff could believe what was unfolding before their eyes, and we hadn't even started.

I took my place at the large, polished wooden table. To my left then clockwise around the table from me were: the translator, the plaintiff's counsel, the judge, a court clerk, a female intern (who thought she would benefit from this experience), the French court reporter and stenographer, a French lawyer, Ms Corbin (the defence counsel's lawyer from Paris), and finally Connor Sears and Jason Harmon for Sanofi, their two lawyers from Shook, Hardy and Bacon. I looked at them and wondered if they had really wanted to do this, if their boss just picked them, or if they had volunteered. A freebie to Toulouse, France, who would want to turn that offer down? I was surprised their boss didn't want to do this.

The introductions began, and the judge announced that the UK court reporter had missed her second flight down to Toulouse and wouldn't join us until lunchtime. This was a good start.

The judge introduced herself to me and explained how Judge North (in the USA) asked her to conduct this deposition. There was a brief discussion about the absence of the videorecording. The plaintiff's counsel had requested my deposition be videotaped; Sanofi had objected. The final decision would be with the French court. I found this odd. It is my understanding that Sanofi videotaped all of the depositions it noticed in the States. Yet, when they had the opportunity to depose me—someone they made a point of silencing for years—they not only chose not to videotape my deposition, but actually object to the plaintiff's lawyer's request to videotape the deposition. Maybe it's just Sanofi's normal practice to object to everything the other side requests.

I was then sworn in. It was off-putting to speak then have to wait for the interpreter to translate it into French and then for the French to reply then be translated back into English.

The judge told me, 'I remind you that according to article 434-13 of the Criminal Code of 19 Justice, telling a lie under oath before any jurisdiction or any judiciary officer in the execution of a letter rogatory is sentenced with five years' imprisonment and 75,000 euros fine.'

I wouldn't lie. I couldn't anyway as I was under oath, but when I was told the consequences of telling any lies, it left me uneasy in case I lied without knowing I was doing so. What if my memory was so bad that I answered what I believed was the truth and it wasn't? Pictures of us having to sell our house and me being carted off to prison for five years flashed through my mind. I intended to concentrate fully about each and every question, and I would absolutely NOT be answering any question unless I fully understood it. How dare Sanofi put me in this position? *I need to stay alert and fully focused. Please, fruit, behave in my already churning stomach.*

The hearing was being audio recorded. There was more talk about the missing UK court reporter/stenographer, and the judge said, 'I make note of this difficulty. I regret this difficulty as Sanofi could have organised things better.' This made me smile. I got the impression the judge regretted not allowing the videorecording to take place. Did I notice a slight squirm from the defence counsel when she said that?

On the desk in front of the defence team were mountainous piles of files, crammed full of paperwork. Everyone discussed how the hours of questioning were going to be divided. This was going to be an AWFULLY long day.

Mr Sears jumped straight in by asking me if I'd had any conversations with the lawyers for the plaintiff. *Mind your own business.* Then he moved on to my relationship with the plaintiff's counsel. He continued with question after question about them: what we had spoken about, what documents I'd given them, and what were the names of the lawyers I'd met. I couldn't remember what individual documents I'd given them last year. He then asked me how many conversations I'd had with the plaintiff's lawyers. I had no idea.

'Is it possible that you have talked to the plaintiff's lawyers in America 500 times?' he asked.

I wanted to scream at him to shut up and get on with things instead of this obsession he seemed to have about my association with the plaintiff's lawyers.

After what seemed like at least thirty minutes of wasted time, he turned his attention to the documents I'd brought for them. *Oh my God, here we go. Keep cool, you can do this.* I could feel the palpitations as we broached the subject of what I'd brought with me. I explained I had various bits of paperwork and the other information was on a memory stick.

'Do you have that with you now?' he asked.

I told him it was in my bag.

'Would you be able to get it?'

I wasn't parting with my memory stick unless the judge ordered me to. I looked at her while willing myself to go through with it. I could feel Stella urging me on. 'Sock it to them, Shirley. You've got this!' I cleared my throat.

'I object to handing these emails to the defendants under the French Data Protection Act.' There, I'd started, so there was no turning back now.

I went on to say I had prepared something I'd like to give to the judge explaining why I didn't believe Sanofi lawyers should be allowed to obtain the emails from me. That they were private conversations of depressed women discussing their health, their medical care, and they only had these conversations because they believed that they were completely secure and safe. I asked the judge if she would allow me to retrieve this letter from my bag. The look on the faces of the Sanofi team was priceless. This had obviously blindsided them which confused me. If anything, I would have assumed they would be expecting it. Even their French counterpart looked shell-shocked.

I handed over the letter which stated:

'I'm here at the court without the benefit of judicial counsel or any representation. I was asked to release information that is extremely personal and private. None of this information, as far as I know, will help in this case apart from the documents that have already been published and that both parties already have in their possession. I tried to get an authorisation in order to publish the content of the messages of the private group with a view to the success of these proceedings. Messages from all the women that belong to this support group. They all knew that it was a private group and that the information released would remain confidential. I am extremely worried about the fact that I may be acting or speaking to their detriment and to mine, by simply giving this information to the court. Therefore, I will ask for an independent court that an independent lawyer be appointed, and this lawyer will examine the content of these private messages, and they will decide what can be communicated and what has to be protected according to the French law on data protection. I am willing to answer questions on my own person and my own publications. I think this is just a fishing operation aimed at vulnerable people. People that are vulnerable because of their disease. It is important that a person with an extremely good knowledge of French law inform the court of what could be released or not. Therefore, I respectfully ask for the protection of the magistrate in this business.'

The defence team was whispering frantically together, and their French lawyer, Ms Corbin, was scrolling on her phone, no doubt searching the data protection laws. I wanted to punch the air. I got the impression the judge was intrigued by what was turning into the most bizarre situation in her courtroom. I bet the intern was enthralled by it all.

Mr Sears said they had an objection to the documents not being produced. They were conducting research and would make an argument after lunch. They had spent months applying for this deposition through the various courts. It was rather arrogant of them to think they could waltz over to France, and that I would just willingly hand over these private and personal conversations without any resistance.

I did, however, provide both sides with the paperwork that I was prepared to give, but as the papers were all jumbled up in a beautifully disorganised fashion, this caused confusion and killed a good few minutes. I desperately wanted it to be lunchtime. The French love their two-hour lunch, but we weren't going to enjoy that on this occasion.

The questioning from Mr Sears turned to my failed attempt in 2011 for compensation through the CRCI, which is similar to a medical injuries board. I explained how it would never go in my favour as the CRCI kept stalling with my application, and even though I had blamed the drug Taxotere, they put my claim against Sanofi.

Back in 2011, given that Sanofi said this adverse side effect of permanent hair loss was very rare and, according to my oncologist, I was only the third or fourth person in the world to suffer from it, I was amazed that suddenly the CRCI managed to find an 'expert' on the subject in Paris. His first words after asking me to remove my headscarf were, 'That certainly looks like it's caused by Taxotere.' Nodding his head, he suddenly added that my hair loss might be caused by other factors that happened several years after my treatment ended. This made no sense, because Sanofi itself said that if hair hadn't regrown after six months, we should realise it wasn't going to.

A female Sanofi lawyer started having an embarrassing shouting tantrum during my session with the CRCI. It ended up with the CRCI expert telling her that if she ever got breast cancer, he hoped she wouldn't have to have Taxotere. That silenced her immediately. The expert said I would have to have a scalp biopsy before my case went any further. That never materialised, even after I enquired about it many times. I knew they were just going through the motions so they could close my case. Heaven forbid they set a precedent to all the other potential breast cancer patients suing for the same problem. When my case eventually came before a committee, who were tired after a long day of hearings, the magistrate refused to allow me to read out my short statement even though she let Sanofi read theirs; it was obvious which way it was going to go. When the Sanofi lawyer read his statement, it came out that when I had my treatment, Taxotere was used off-label, and because my oncologist hadn't informed me about this, it was a perfect excuse for the magistrate to shift the blame away from Sanofi by blaming my oncologist and not the drug.

But back to the deposition. Mr Sears opened one of the files and produced an email or part of an email that I had written to the support group. *Oh, God. Which embarrassing one is this going to be?* There were so many rants, I was dreading them being produced in court. I cringed and had a hot flash.

Yes, it was one of *THOSE*!

I nearly died in my seat as he read out what I'd written:

'In frustration, I went to Paris and sprayed graffiti on Sanofi HQ. That was the greatest thrill of all. Hmm, what else? Oh yes! Much to Sally's disgust, I made a YouTube video of me taking the mickey out of Sanofi and then mooned at them.'

Looking over at the judge for a reaction, especially to the graffiti incident, I noticed she displayed an exceptionally good poker face. But I'm sure I saw a twinkle in her eye.

Really, what was the point of reading that message out other than to humiliate me? Was this the way a company that describes itself as 'chasing the miracles of science to improve people's lives' holds itself out? Try and humiliate any patient that dares to criticise your product? It had the desired effect. Nice one, Sanofi.

Mr Sears then mentioned that I'd recorded the meeting with the expert, Sanofi's lawyers, and its doctor without anyone's consent.

OK, I have thick skin. Sock it to me, Mr Sears. Do your best.

He fired many questions at me which I couldn't answer or didn't fully understand, and I had to keep asking him to rephrase them. I could see that each time I asked him to do this, Ms Corbin sighed and looked like she was getting impatient. I certainly wasn't trying to waste time, but given the consequence the judge had explained to me if I lied, I wasn't going to answer a question I didn't fully understand. If she didn't like that, tough. I didn't care.

He turned his attention to asking me about the different law firms that had purchased my book *Naked in the Wind* then had contacted me, and the articles I had written for them.

There was one question I could not understand at all. I had no idea what he was trying to ask. Eventually, when we were getting nowhere, Ms Corbin spoke up.

'Sorry, I believe that the questions are clear, and the witness is deliberately not answering them. And I would like to ask you to please request from the witness that she answers the question even if she doesn't see the purpose of it.'

The plaintiff's counsel, Karen Menzies, tried to explain that some of the questions had to do with American legal terms and terminology and that they were vague as to time, etc. and she thought I was doing my best to respond.

Ms Corbin retaliated. 'If you allow me to answer, Madame Menzies does not represent Madame Ledlie. The objections are just formal and for the American judge, and the witness has come here to answer the questions that she is asked. So, I maintain my request.'

Ooops!

She must still have been unhappy from my objection to handing over my precious stash earlier in the day.

The judge then tried to understand and rephrase the question for me, but the plaintiff's council stated no, that wasn't a correct interpretation. She seemed as clueless as me to what Mr Sears was asking.

Thankfully, the judge then announced it was time for lunch. We would start again in one hour. At that point, I didn't know how I would get through the afternoon if this line of questioning continued.

CHAPTER SEVEN

An Arduous Afternoon

After lunch, the UK court reporter arrived. I couldn't help but feel sorry for her; she must have felt so embarrassed.

Mr Sears started with his favourite obsessive topic, asking me if I'd spoken to the plaintiff's counsel over the lunch break. He then asked the judge to clarify the allotted time for the rest of the afternoon. After another glance at the pile of paperwork they obviously wanted to get through, it was plain as day it was never going to happen.

The thought of an afternoon of being given the third degree and staring at the files on the desk depleted my energy reserves. Because every question consisted of me having to wait for the interpreter to translate into French, I had to try to remember not to answer immediately in case the plaintiff's counsel wanted to say, 'object to form'. My head was bobbing from side to side like a tennis ball at the French Open. By the time it was right for me to answer the question, I'd often already forgotten what it was. There was often talk between the lawyers, too, which all helped to push those clock hands around.

Mr Sears then asked me if I'd heard of, or had contact with, Dr Tosti and Dr Miteva. Their names were not familiar to me.

'Are you aware there is a reference to you in a study that Dr Tosti and Dr Miteva wrote?' he asked.

That was news to me!

The documents that were going to be presented next were covered by a protective order delivered by the American judge. The Shook, Hardy and Bacon lawyers stated that I would have to sign one.

After a quick discussion, the plaintiff's counsel said, 'The protective order that has been entered in this case Ms Ledlie has signed, so she is permitted to see documents—internal documents—that have been produced by Sanofi.' The surprised look on the three defence lawyers' faces was fun to see. It fed their curiosity. It was eventually agreed that Mr Sears would receive a copy of the paperwork I'd signed long ago. And again, I thought I detected an element of surprise on the judge's face. *I think she's enjoying this.*

I glanced at the clock. It was surprising how quickly time was moving on. Now it was the turn of the plaintiff's counsel, Ms Menzies, to question me. Relief swept over me.

We addressed many of the documents Mr Sears had already questioned me about. It was to clarify that I had no way of knowing whether any of them was a complete email exchange. For all I knew, these conversations within the support group that he'd referred to could have been copied and pasted by the Shook, Hardy and Bacon lawyers, maybe sections removed, taking everything out of context. I understood why this part of the questioning could be important. After being shown an exhibit, I was repeatedly asked if I had given this document to Sanofi's counsel. The answer was always no. I hadn't given them anything, nor would I if I had anything to do with it.

As Ms Menzies was wrapping up, she said, 'You chose not to wear your wig today, and I understand that is unusual. Can you explain why you decided to do that?' Mr Sears objected to this question. I was glad to hear a reference to my appearance and also confused as to why Mr Sears could possibly object.

'I wanted everybody in the room to know, to remember throughout the day, why we are here.'

Oh God, more questioning from 'them' next.

Mr Sears started by asking about the protective order I'd signed with the plaintiff's counsel in 2018, and what mobile phone provider I was with. Why on earth did he want to know which provider I used?

Then it got fun!

The subject turned to the Data Protection Act.

Mr Sears: 'How did you find out about data privacy laws?'

Me: 'A friend told me about them.'

Mr Sears: 'Is your friend a lawyer?'

Me: 'No.' I bet that answer disappointed him.

Mr Sears: 'Is your friend French?'

Me: 'No.'

Mr Sears: 'Where does your friend live?'

Me: 'France.' I wanted to add, 'Sorry to disappoint you, but she doesn't live in the USA.' It seemed like such a waste of his time to keep questioning me about this, but that suited me. He could waste as much time as he wanted.

Mr Sears: 'How did you get into a discussion with

your friend about data privacy laws?'

I suppose he could have asked me if my friend was a retired criminal barrister, or if my friend's daughter was a law student. I guess you have to ask the right questions.

It was now almost 5:30 p.m., and the deposition was finally coming to an end, thank God. The judge explained that she wasn't going to make a decision that day about my objecting to handing over the memory stick, and we would have to remain patient and wait till the following Thursday. I couldn't help but feel confident she would come to the right decision. In fact, I didn't think the GDPA could be twisted in any shape or form to suit Sanofi's entitled demand. The look of disbelief and disappointment on the Shook, Hardy and Bacon team's faces was priceless.

The thought of the two Sanofi lawyers flying back to the USA empty handed after an expensive exercise made me feel as though I'd won the lottery, but the best was yet to come.

On April 18th, the judge issued an order rejecting the request to produce documents. If you had peeked through our windows, you would have witnessed this nutty half bald woman running around the house punching the air, whooping, and clapping. Yes, we seem to have many 'running around the house moments' at home.

I had this mental image of whoever the Sanofi lawyers' boss was back at their office in Kansas not being a happy bunny, telling them what a waste of time and money that was. I felt a little sorry for Mr Sears as I think he was taken aback by the amount of people in the room, a few in formal attire, as I'm sure that's not how it's done back in the States. Plus, it's possible he thought that with my volatile reputation, I'd be screaming and hurling abuse at him. Let's face it, he only had my ranty, sweary emails and memoir to go by, so who could blame him for expecting this patient gone rogue. Hey, I didn't care. They lost. I won! Woop, woop.

My celebration didn't last long as the courthouse contacted me and explained that Sanofi's defence team had appealed against the judge's decision. I prayed it would still stand as it seemed to fall well within the protection of the GDPR. Time would tell.

CHAPTER EIGHT
Expenses

After sending my deposition expenses invoice and bank details to Shook, Hardy and Bacon, I forgot about them. After all, it was official business, and I had no reason to doubt the payment would be made, and pronto.

So why did reimbursements totalling less than two hundred euros become a battle of wills between a disgruntled deponent, a law firm working for one the of world's largest drug companies, and not one but two judges? They'd just spent thousands on the exercise to get, well, nothing from the deposition, and now they didn't want to pay me less than two hundred euros for the pleasure. It reeked of pettiness. Did they really want to go into combat for the sake of a couple of hundred euros, especially as they know me, or think they do? Never underestimate the strength of a woman. Remember Helen Reddy!

I lost track of the number of times I requested payment from them and was ignored. *Right, what's next, Shirley? Think.*

I emailed the Toulouse judge's office, explained what was happening, or not happening, and asked that Shook, Hardy and Bacon's appeal be put on hold by the court until they abided by the French law Article 748 and paid me what they owe.

I also emailed the American court, Judge North's office, to report Shook, Hardy and Bacon's silent refusal to pay their debt. I waited. And waited. Still nothing, so I emailed the US judge yet again. Still nothing. Surely Judge North must have instructed them to pay, and yet they still refused? OK, I understand they don't like me much, but this was supposed to be a professional company. They had to know payment was required and that they would be forced into it in the end.

Ping—you've got mail. The deposition transcript, which had previously been delayed, was now ready and waiting for me. I had to return to the city centre courthouse and sign for it. The email also stated Shook, Hardy and Bacon had dropped the appeal against my small but significant win; it was great to hear they had come to their senses. A victory for the little people, albeit a small one. So, I suppose you could say their plan to obtain my emails was foiled by a budding law student. They need to seriously think about hiring Teddy.

I went to sign for the transcript and was immediately ushered into the judge's office. After completing that little task, I explained my expenses were still unpaid even after many emails to Shook, Hardy and Bacon and the American judge; my requests had seemingly fallen on deaf ears. She did not look amused and vanished after telling me not to leave her office. Five minutes later she reappeared with a document and asked me for the total amount I was owed. I added another twenty euros for that day's parking. Signing and stamping the paper, she told me to post it, recorded delivery, to Ms Corbin in Paris, and

Sanofi WOULD pay it, immediately. Three days later, the full amount was in my bank account.

CHAPTER NINE
Another Day

With everything now finally over as far as I was concerned, I was excited at the thought of concentrating on my gardening. I was still annoyed that Sanofi had tried to get me banned from Facebook. Each time I thought about it, I could feel my blood pressure rise; that was why my garden was looking so good. It was the only place I could forget this nightmare.

One beautiful afternoon I was busy in the greenhouse, music playing through my phone, and I was in my happy place. The birds were furiously feeding on the ancient, dilapidated bird table when the music stopped. Squinting at the screen without my glasses, looking for another Motown album, I accidentally clicked on my Hotmail account. There was something from an unknown address. I assumed it was spam, but I checked anyway. Good job I did.

A lawyer, Ivan, introduced himself to me and asked if he could call me as he wanted to pick my brain about Taxotere. This had now become the story of my life. Of course, I'm always happy to help in any way I can.

We chatted, and he explained he was working for a lady suffering from permanent hair loss after having Taxotere. He wanted to help her as she didn't have an easy home life and now had this nightmare to cope with. I listened to her moving story and offered to help in any way I could. I answered his questions, asking him to let me know the outcome. The litigation was against the clinic that had treated her and was not connected to the Sanofi lawsuits.

Not long passed before I heard from Ivan again. He asked me if I'd be willing to make a short video explaining how this adverse side effect had affected my life so he could use it to help his client's case. I set to work and sent it off to him, asking him to keep me posted.

Then something unexpected happened.

The Paxman Scalp Cooling company, who I've been in touch with for several years, contacted me. I had previously interviewed their CEO for The Cancer Hub on my personal website. Their device is used during chemotherapy sessions to help women keep their hair throughout treatment, and it also promotes a quicker regrowth after chemotherapy has finished. Anyway, they were making a promotional video, and they wanted to touch on the subject of permanent hair loss, and of course, that's where I came in. I got John to take three or four painfully close-up headshots, and I sent them off. They promised to send me a copy of the video before it went live.

Sometime later, I received a YouTube link and pressed play. Oh God, the tears flowed like Niagara flippin' falls as I watched these ladies talk about when they first learnt of their breast cancer diagnosis and how the thought of losing their hair made them feel. The music and the commentator's voice were beautiful and compassionate, full of true understanding. The video then showed their hair after chemotherapy had finished and the results of using this scalp cooling device. Their hair looked amazing. I was sobbing by this stage. *Why wasn't I allowed this when I asked my oncologist? Why was she so quick to say, no, it didn't work with Taxotere*? When I received chemotherapy, Taxotere had only been used for early-stage breast cancer for six months, so how could she know it wouldn't work? There would be no data after six months.

The video turned to the subject of permanent hair loss, and my headshots came on screen. I was now a blubbering wreck. It set the scene nicely for a full-day pity party.

I was still full of self-pity the next morning. The video had been dispiriting for me and had opened a deep wound. I couldn't stop asking myself why my oncologist refused me the use of the scalp cooling device; why, why, why? I only asked her verbally, so if I questioned her about it now, she would only deny it. *Just let it go, Shirley*.

That day was a real struggle until late afternoon when I got a surprise phone call from the lawyer, Ivan, who I'd sent the video to in order to try and help the lady he was working for. He was excited to tell me that the clinic had settled out of court. This was fantastic news, and I was so pleased for the lady in question and for Ivan. This was exactly what I needed to hear. It will never bring her hair back, of course, but at least she could now afford to buy the best wigs or afford help with her life in some other way.

A very British tradition was called for. I put the kettle on and had a large mug of tea. I sat down with my drink in the shade of our terrace, surrounded by swaying bushes of fragrant lemongrass and intense red canna lilies, the tea warming my soul. I thought about all the amazing, caring, and incredibly talented people I'd got to know throughout this whole bizarre story. It was a very humbling moment.

CHAPTER TEN
Next on the List

The litigation in the USA was getting under way. There were going to be six bellwether trials. As I understand it, these trials are used to predict ranges of what a representative jury might award a plaintiff, and hopefully give both sides a better idea of what a compensatory settlement might look like. This is what I have drawn from what I have read on DocketBird.

I so desperately wanted to go to one of these trials, trying to imagine how these women would feel sitting in a witness box with *this* hair and looking out at the sea of faces staring back at them. The jurors could be thinking, 'My mother died of breast cancer, and you sit there trying to sue for your hair not growing back. I wouldn't care if my mum had terrible hair like yours as long as she was alive.' I suppose it would be so easy for people to have these thoughts, but this isn't what this is about. It's about patients' rights; it's about transparency from pharmaceutical companies; it's about giving informed consent for your treatment, whatever that treatment is for. It's about quality of life and not being permanently disfigured because the pharmaceutical company wanted to make billions of dollars. It's about having to live with a permanent disfigurement and a permanent reminder that you have had cancer.

And finally, it's about the company, in this case Sanofi. There is no doubt that Sanofi is in the pharmaceutical business to make money, and it makes a LOT of it. Sanofi is reported to be the fourth largest pharmaceutical company in the world, with revenues in 2019 of over $42,000,000,000 and profits of over $14,000,000,000 (source: www.fortune.com/company/sanofi/global500).

But that should not absolve Sanofi from truthfully and accurately communicating what it knows about the risks of its Taxotere drug. Knowing that it could cause this disfiguring side effect but keeping it hidden, hoping to keep a lid on it for as long as possible, all the while raking in billions in sales is unconscionable. What makes it even worse is there has always been an equally if not more effective taxane (Taxol) that does not have the same risk as Taxotere; it's all about choice.

The first bellwether trial came and went with a verdict for the defence. I was so disappointed. I thought about the plaintiff and plaintiff's counsel and how they would be feeling, especially those I'd previously met, like Karen Menzies and David Miceli. I know that they, and the rest of their team, are fighting a good fight to hold Sanofi responsible for not being truthful with patients like me.

I started a GoFundMe campaign to raise money to enable several support group members to attend the trials. How brilliant it would be for the woman whose trial it is to see that kind of support in the public gallery, especially during cross-examination. I set about my plan which included taking part in a live video on my author Facebook page. I had to do it live, or I would be forever stopping and starting, and I haven't a clue how to begin editing a video. If I wore a hat, nobody would know what I was talking about; they would see hair sticking out of the bottom and not appreciate that in reality I look like an orangutan.

I was really nervous thinking about doing it, but I wanted to try. Anyway, what was the worst that could happen? I could cock it up and look an idiot. Well, I already have the T-shirt for that, many times over, and wear it with pride. I made the video and was blown away by people's generosity and kindness; it quickly reached over 3,000 views.

Then Covid-19 struck, and we all know what happened following that.

Eventually the trial date for the second bellweather trial was set. The plaintiff was Elizabeth Kahn, and I booked my flight to the US.

It was impossible to contact the support group without Sanofi lawyers seeing my post, and I didn't want to alert them that I was making plans to go. I envisaged them begging the judge to close the public gallery because of Covid-19 or other desperate excuses, anything to keep me out, and they had no way of knowing how many baldies I would bring along with me. I doubted they would want the jury to see another victim of this drug under the same roof. It was so frustrating not being able to tell the support group girls; damn Shook, Hardy and Bacon for ruining our private place, our sanctuary. Hardly the behaviour you expect from a company that boasts: 'from our beginning as a local French enterprise to our position as a leading global healthcare company, reinvention is in our DNA and reflects our quest to make life better for patients…' The company's never-ending quest to silence women that raise concern over its blessed Taxotere only deepens the offence. Sanofi knew, and it didn't warn vulnerable women. But I digress.

Back to my plans. I would just have to go by myself. I put plans in motion and packed my bag. It was hilarious, because when I told my children and Mum that I was going over to attend the trial, the first thing they all separately said was, 'They might try to run you down or have you shot.'

New Orleans, here I come.

CHAPTER ELEVEN
Arrival in New Orleans

John was on his way home from a business trip in the USA the same day my alarm woke me up at four thirty to leave for the airport. I needed a calm stomach, but mine was churning like a washing machine going in for its final spin cycle. The thought of three flights to get to New Orleans with not a great deal of time left for a change at Atlanta was incredibly stressful for me. I would soon panic if I got lost, especially at an unfamiliar airport. *Get on with it, you wimp*.

As previously arranged with John, I left my car for him to drive home that lunchtime when his flight landed. When I walked into the airport departures terminal, the reality of what I was doing hit me. *I'm flying to the USA on my own to attend a trial and with nothing on my head. Am I insane? What am I thinking*? I had no luggage to hand in; travelling light does have benefits, but the main reason for my lack of bags was I was worried my luggage wouldn't arrive, and as the trial was the following morning, I desperately needed my clothes. Who goes to the USA not taking empty suitcases for shopping? Would there even be time to hit the shops?

It was a short flight to Paris, and then I had a couple of hours' wait for my connection. There was no rushing and getting all hot and sweaty, so all was going to plan, so far.

I felt strangely calm as I took my seat for the flight to Atlanta. *This is it, too late to change my mind now.*

I'd dreamt about doing this, and it was finally happening. The hours flew (sorry) by as I ate meals, watched mind-numbing rubbish on the screen and had a sleep, thanks to taking my memory foam neck cushion, and we started to make our descent into Atlanta. The flight from Paris had departed thirty minutes late, so that left it tight for me to get my next flight to New Orleans.

I could feel my panic rising as they announced security were waiting at the plane's door to check our PCR test papers. We hardly moved for ten minutes, and I guessed by then I was going to miss my next flight. Another ten minutes went by, and suddenly we were on the move; they'd given up with that idea. I ran with my bags falling off my shoulder and neck cushion ending up on the floor more times than I care to remember. I stopped to catch my breath and looked down at the never-ending line of gate numbers in front of me, and yes, of course, mine was the very last one. With trembling legs and drenched in sweat, I eventually made it to my gate. A group of staff was chatting; nobody else was there. The plane had taken off minutes before.

I took a slow walk back up past the gates and found the Delta Air Lines enquiry desk. Luckily, there was another flight to New Orleans two hours later. We were crammed on like sardines, but I didn't care. I was almost there. I spent the next one and a half hours with my eyes closed, going over the last sixteen years since my cancer diagnosis: what an odyssey they had turned into. Was this the pinnacle? But as has happened so many times before, when I think I've reached the end of the road and have a short, quiet spell, something always sets the wheels in motion again.

The eagle had landed, and I disembarked at the Louis Armstrong New Orleans Airport, fully charged with empowerment.

My taxi pulled up outside the Drury Inn around 10 p.m. After signing in and telling them I didn't want housekeeping all week (I was worried about catching COVID from touching surfaces), I was given my key. The week before, I'd emailed the hotel and asked if there was an option for wheat-free bread with their breakfast; if not, I would try to squash a small loaf in my luggage. I didn't hear back from them, but as it happened there was definitely not enough space in my bags, so I'd manage without.

'Oh, Mrs Ledlie, before you go up to your room, I have something for you,' the front desk assistant shouted just as I was about to get in the lift.

If it's an envelope, should I accept it? I doubt it'll be anything I'll be happy about.

As I reached the reception desk, he was holding a loaf of wheat-free bread, a present from the manager. How thoughtful.

My room was nice with a huge bed and a mountain of soft pillows plus one of those lovely snuggly quilts so many hotels have. I put my bags on a table, got out my large packet of sanitising wipes and set to work. An hour later, I'd finished. I showered and sent John a message to say I'd arrived safely. It was just before midnight, and I collapsed into bed. Going by French time, it was 7 a.m. I lay in bed and put my phone on charge and was just setting the alarm when John FaceTimed me, and we chatted for a while.

I woke seconds before the alarm and called John. A hot shower helped wake me up and the soap dispenser on the wall also had hair conditioner in, so I used it. Don't ask me why I thought that was a clever idea. But it was there, so I did. I got dressed and put my make-up on. My power make-up look! I needed confidence by the bucketload if I was to go through with my plan.

Grabbing my face mask and a couple of slices of my bread, I headed downstairs to find the breakfast room. It was spaciously laid out, and there was an excellent choice. I was soon back in my room to brush my teeth, put a notebook in my handbag, and head off in the direction of the courthouse, but not before placing a bin in a position behind my door so I would know if anyone had gone into my room while I was out.

Once in the street, I seemed to be the only one wearing a face mask. Oh well. As I'd checked out the location on Google Earth umpteen times at home, I felt as though I'd already walked down this road, many times. In less than a ten-minute walk, I recognised the large grey building on the right. The Hale Boggs Federal Building and Courthouse, 500 Poydras Street, was set back from the pavement, and trees hid the offices that ran alongside the main entrance. I walked between the trees and court offices and removed my turban. Looking at my reflection in the windows was startling for me let alone anyone looking out of their window while enjoying their morning coffee. The hair conditioner I used that morning had made my hair floaty, as though the breeze was whispering to it.

Walking alongside the building, I could see a queue

of people at the end. The feeling of dread increased with every step. *Are they all going to turn around and stare at me?* I felt naked (*Naked in The Wind*) as I joined the end of the line without a single person giving me a second glance. *Phew*! When the entrance and security came into sight, I could see everyone taking it in turn to stand in front of a camera as they entered the doors, then joining another much smaller queue before being called into the security zone one at a time. It was soon my turn. I obediently stood on the large X, pulling my mask down and ensuring my face fit into the yellow square on the screen. A loud 'thank you' boomed out with each photo it took.

The security guy called out for me to enter, place my bag on the counter, and show him my vaccination certificate. His expression amused me as he could only understand the document had a QR code.

'What language is this?' he asked, bemused.

'French. I live in France.'

He waved me through the metal detector machine, and I waited at the other end for my bag to reappear on the conveyor belt. He stuck a fluorescent green sticker on me to say I was screened.

I turned right, as that was where everyone was going, and a woman was guiding people into the correct elevators. I headed in her direction. After I told her the judge's name, she pointed at an elevator, advising me to use it, get out on the first floor, and turn left. I pressed the button to the first floor, and just as the doors were closing, a young blonde woman squeezed through, huffing, puffing, and muttering to herself. Smiling to myself, I assumed she was running late for work. She vanished as soon as the doors opened, and I followed the instructions of the guide downstairs. It was a long, carpeted hallway, with various wooden doors on both sides. At the far end were large posters displaying local history. Floor-to-ceiling windows provided views down to the street below. *Look for a plaque with Judge Milazzo's name on. Here it is; doesn't look much like a courtroom door, but anyway…*

I gingerly opened the door and entered a narrow, plush-looking corridor with doors either side where muffled voices were seeping through. *This can't be right.* I turned and fled back to where I'd gone in. After rummaging around in my bag and jacket pockets to find my glasses, I read the plaque, and to my utter horror realised it was the judge's private chambers. The relief I felt at not being discovered in there! How would I have explained that one?

Back out in the main corridor, it was silent, nobody there to see my awkward and very embarrassed exit. I walked on to the next door. These large double wooden doors looked more like what I was expecting, and a sign outside indicated I was finally in the right place.

Because of the potential horror of being caught wandering around Judge Milazzo's private chambers, I didn't have time to compose myself or worry about entering the courtroom, which was definitely a good thing. In I walked. Of course, heads turned, especially from Sanofi's side, and I can only assume that because I hadn't been there for the first week of the trial, they didn't expect me to show up. Well, I did, and here I was.

I took my place on the plaintiff's side and on a ridiculously hard wooden bench and straight away noticed Elizabeth Kahn, whose trial it was. We exchanged looks and a little nod.

Now, I have a well-padded derrière, but even that didn't protect me from the intense hardness of the bench. *Christ, how can I sit on this all day?* I had to remove my thin jacket and fold it up to create a meagre cushion, wishing I'd travelled over in my thick winter coat. The seating problem was half solved, but the air conditioner high up on my side of the wall was blowing out a sub-zero blast. Was it set so cold to keep everyone alert? Looking around the large courtroom, I could see the jury's nicely padded seating was right in front of where I was sitting.

Taking my notebook out, I quickly made a sketch of the courtroom's layout. We were allowed to have our phones on, but they must be on silent, and no photos were allowed, which was a real shame. I double-checked my phone was on silent; I doubted the Star Trek theme ringtone would have gone down too well with the court.

People came and went then suddenly there was a knocking on the far end door, next to the judge's seat.

All rise.

Once Judge Milazzo was seated, we all sat back down. It wasn't long before a court staff member shouted for us to all rise as the jurors filtered in one at a time. There was the blonde lady that had got into my elevator.

Because I'd missed the first week, I had no way of knowing how it had ended, but the first witness, Dr Feigal, gave me the impression she was carrying on from the Friday before. Dr Ellen Feigal is an oncologist experienced with clinical trials, pharmacovigilance, and pharmacological product development.

She was direct and feisty; no matter what Sanofi's lawyers threw at her, nothing flustered this expert. The defence tried taking things out of context to impeach her. After objections from the plaintiff's counsel and some pauses for sidebars (an area in a courtroom where lawyers may be called to speak off the record with the judge without being overheard by the jury), the defence lawyers got nowhere. Amongst other things, they discussed the Bradford Hill Causation Criteria, assessment of quality-of-life treatment and outcomes of patients, studies TAX316, TAX301, study BCIRG005, and labelling. Much of this evidence was complicated, but I stayed alert thanks to the arctic blast and hard bench. Amongst other things, I learnt that no placebos are used in oncology trials. Of course, it makes perfect sense. You need to treat cancer, so you can't give a person a placebo.

It was a relief when we broke for lunch, and I dashed down the road to the hotel to grab a snack. When I'd finished breakfast that morning, I had taken up a container of butter and cheese as there was a fridge in the room, so I was able to make a sandwich and give John a quick call before heading back to the courthouse for the afternoon's session.

The ten-minute walk back didn't go without incident. The pavement was wide, and there were not many pedestrians about, but I spotted a group of men heading in my direction. As they got closer, it looked like four guys in their thirties or forties walking with their elderly father. They were all big strapping men, and the father was strolling along with his hands stuffed deeply into his jean pockets. My eyes darted down to the pavement and noticed a large piece of slab missing, directly in front of the presumed father. Before I could shout, 'Watch out,' to him, he tripped and hit the ground with a thud, face first, rendering him unconscious. *Oh my God.* My natural instinct was to run over to see if I could help, but the sons were all gathered around him. One thanked me, saying two of the brothers were paramedics, so my very rustic first aid skills weren't needed. I felt sick. As I reached the courthouse, I looked back and could see them helping their father to sit down on a wall and what looked like blood down the front of his shirt. Poor man. So, remember never to walk with your hands in your pockets.

By now I didn't feel great but wasn't sure if it was from the shock of seeing that man hitting the deck or because jet lag had set in, but whichever it was, the freezing blast from the air conditioner was welcome that afternoon.

I took my seat on the front bench again and saw what I assumed to be the plaintiff's husband sitting next to one of her lawyers. He looked like a kind gentleman, and I hoped taking the stand this afternoon wouldn't be too tough on him. He was there to support his wife, and I know from personal experience that when a woman suffers from this adverse side effect, the whole family suffers, not just the woman. Preparing for this case for years must take its toll on everyone.

All rise.

The previous witness, Dr Feigal, was still giving evidence, talking about patients' quality of life and treatment outcomes.

Even though it was not long since lunchtime, I had to choose whether to freeze to death to save the butt pain or put my coat on and have no cushion. I decided to take my chances of suffering from hypothermia.

Next up was Elizabeth's husband. As he walked over to the witness box, my hands were clenched. I took this minute's break to find a tissue, one that was dry as all the others were wet from wiping the dew drops dripping from my frost-bitten nose.

I was already feeling very emotional, and he hadn't even started. My frequent glances over to the jury didn't exactly instil confidence in me, and it was disappointing to see only two of the eight were taking occasional notes. A couple of them looked as though they were having trouble staying awake despite the freezing temperature as they were slouched down in comfy chairs with their thick bomber jackets pulled up around their ears. Another juror kept looking around the courtroom and glancing over at the clock at least every five minutes. However, all their attention was now focused on Elizabeth's husband.

He was questioned about the blogs Elizabeth kept while having treatment and how he authored some of them. He seemed a warm and compassionate man, and it looked as though the jurors liked him. Even though they didn't have partners suffering from permanent hair loss, there on the stand was a husband, a caring partner with a sense of humour instead of academic witnesses explaining data which was hard to grasp, especially when they used medical terminology that was very likely to be mind-numbing to people that weren't even interested in the subject in the first place.

The Sanofi team showed photographs of holiday

snaps from Elizabeth's blogs where she was posing and smiling. They were obviously trying to make out that if you were depressed, you couldn't smile and that she was still enjoying her life. They were undoubtedly relying on the jurors to have no awareness of the smiling depression where the sufferer portrays enjoying a happy life on the outside while living with depression on the inside.

Elizabeth's husband was asked how living with permanent hair loss from her treatment had affected his wife. I immediately pictured John up there and what he would say. If I'm brutally honest, I think it was a bit of a missed opportunity; there was surely so much more that he could have said, but it's easy to say when it's not you in the witness box. He seemed such a genuine man, and the love he showed for his wife was easy to see. I believed the jury must be taken with him. Anyway, my floodgates opened, and the tears flowed. I just couldn't stop, no matter how hard I tried. How embarrassing. It was incredibly emotional.

He left the stand. The defence team then objected to a comment Elizabeth's husband made, and the judge instructed the jurors to disregard it. The afternoon break couldn't have come at a more appropriate time, giving me ten minutes or so to try and compose myself.

After the much-needed break came the charismatic, Irish-American statistician and academic, David Madigan. His résumé was remarkable, and he spoke with a captivating, gentle, lilting Irish brogue. He had the jury's full attention. Who knew that meta-analysis could be so fascinating? *Why aren't the jurors taking notes?*

The day's session was over…almost. After the

jurors left the courtroom, hushed discussion from the defence team got underway. Suddenly a bombshell detonated. Shook, Hardy and Bacon announced they were going to try their luck and ask for a mistrial based on a particular comment Elizabeth's husband made. Although I didn't think for one minute their ploy was going to work, when it comes to dealing with Sanofi you can be sure to expect the unexpected. Judge Milazzo announced that she would make her decision and meet with both counsels in her chambers at 8 a.m. the next morning. *I'd better make sure I take the right door in the morning then.*

It felt great to stand up, stretch my legs and rub my butt, not to mention put my coat on. As I walked out past security, the late afternoon air felt warm and muggy, and that was fine by me. I made my way back to the hotel; it was only 5 p.m., but already dusk wasn't far away.

Back in the room, it felt great kicking off my ankle boots. I hung my clothes up and flopped on the bed with a bottle of ice-cold water and a bag of peanut butter Ritz biscuits, which I've never seen in France. After calling John, I wrote more notes up, got dressed, and went downstairs to eat. The hotel put free food on in the evenings, and guests were entitled to three, yes three, free alcoholic drinks. A big, soft chair in the bar beckoned. I sank down in it while sipping a triple Bombay Sapphire gin and tonic and eating a plate of the best pulled BBQ pork ever.

I grabbed a street map from reception and wandered around a large area of the French Quarter. Before leaving Poydras Street, I picked out a tall building across the road from the hotel to use as a landmark in case I got disorientated. I found myself just wandering down any street that took my fancy, enjoying the sights of the French Quarter, many of which I'd seen on TV. The numerous tourists added to the friendly ambience. I peered down at the ground before stepping off the pavement—Toulouse Street!

After a couple of hours, I returned to the hotel feeling zombified. No matter how sleepy I felt, I couldn't seem to drift off till around midnight. Then at 4 a.m., I woke up starving, my internal clock all confused.

CHAPTER TWELVE
Elizabeth's Day

The same routine followed the next morning. I decided to sit on the Sanofi side of the public gallery in the hope that it wouldn't be quite as cold, being further away from the blowers. As I took a place on their front bench, there were a few looks from the Sanofi team, and it was noticeable they couldn't speak as freely to each other and had to do their chatting further away from the front bench. For the second day, it looked like the public gallery was being used mostly by people involved in the case. I did spot three or four women sitting at the back of the gallery writing notes by hand. They didn't have suits on, so maybe they were journalists? I like to think they were as I had sent out a press release to all the local news outlets to try and drum up as much interest as possible. My scribbled jottings would be undecipherable as my glasses slipped off because of my mandatory face mask each time I looked down, so I gave up with my glasses and scrawled away erratically.

It was definitely less cold on that side of the room.

All rise.

The judge started by saying the request for a mistrial was denied. Thank God for that! The jury was then allowed back in.

The statistician was back on the stand. He covered

a multitude of topics including controlled trials, observational studies, randomised trials, and meta-analysis. I was enthralled. He explained that even though randomised trials are the most efficient, observational studies are still of use. The jurors were paying attention to him intently, or so it seemed, but still nobody was taking notes. Without referring to my journal, I do remember, a year later, that meta-analysis is an analysis of multiple analyses. So, I did learn something.

I had to admire David Madigan; his knowledge was astounding. I couldn't wait for the defence to have their turn. There was no way on this planet they were going to trip the formidable Mr Madigan up or get him flustered, not a hope in hell.

Shook, Hardy and Bacon got their chance and try as they might, failed miserably. They resorted to asking hypothetical questions. Numerous angry-looking sidebars were called by the plaintiff's counsel. Whenever there was a sidebar, piped music played, and that day, we were treated to Louis Armstrong (of course!) and 'What a Wonderful World'. The defence finished by pointing out Mr Madigan was charging seven hundred dollars per hour for court work, trying to infer that he would say whatever the plaintiff's counsel wanted him to say. What a shame the judge had decided that the plaintiff's counsel were not allowed to say how much Sanofi had paid for their Rapid Response Team and the hiring of pharma marketing agency InTouch Solutions in their attempt to shut me up.

It was lunchtime, and it felt so good to get out into the warm sunshine after a tense morning. I'd made a sandwich that morning to save me going back to the hotel, so I walked over to the Benjamin Franklin Park opposite the courthouse, had a picnic, and called John.

All rise.

Elizabeth's husband was in the public gallery, so maybe his wife would take the stand that afternoon. Yikes. I tried to imagine how she must be feeling, but it was impossible. All I knew was I felt sick with nerves.

As Elizabeth took her seat in the witness box, not only did I feel nauseous, but I felt proud of this stranger. This strong woman, who had not only gone through traumatic chemotherapy and discovered she was going to suffer from permanent hair loss, was there to stand up to the oppressors of patients' rights, the enemy—Sanofi! It had taken years for her case to get this far, and she was finally going to have her day in court; no matter what the outcome, she'd be able to hold her head up high.

I can't imagine what damage this kind of stress does to your body, but thank God there are women strong enough to go through it, standing up for what they believe in. Thank God there are lawyers who are prepared to take on the giants of the pharmaceutical world, putting their everything into their work and being a 'voice' for the little people. Without lawyers like Ms Kahn's fighting in her corner, we would be supressed and even more so at the mercy of profiteers like Sanofi.

The session started with the plaintiff's counsel asking questions about Elizabeth's career and her librarian work. Then, high up on the screen, photos of her hair before and after chemotherapy appeared. They asked about her eyebrows, which hadn't grown back, and she removed her glasses to show one she had pencilled in and one that wasn't so that she could show the jury. My heart went out to her.

When it was time for the cross-examination, the atmosphere changed in an instant. The hairs on my arms stood up. I looked across at Elizabeth's husband and wondered how he was coping, watching his wife. Elizabeth stayed strong in her answers. The lawyer, Hildy Sastre, kept repeating that Elizabeth had signed the informed consent form, knowing there were terrible possible adverse side effects. She wanted to know why, if Elizabeth was OK to agree to accept the possibility of these, she now alleged she *wouldn't* have signed if she'd been warned about permanent hair loss. Elizabeth replied repeatedly that she knew she had to have chemotherapy so didn't have a choice. But certain possible side effects are common to all the chemotherapy drugs: temporary hair loss, vomiting, body aches, and—yes—death. Sanofi's lawyers love to talk about death. They said it so often in this trial, you wondered if they were wishing it upon Ms Kahn.

But permanent hair loss, and its *frequency*, is unique to Taxotere. That is what the plaintiff's experts demonstrated, and that is what the science shows us to this day. But Sanofi tries to do its best to hide that truth and confuse the issue that 'cases have been reported' with other chemotherapy drugs. But they know the truth.

At trial there was evidence that Sanofi had been discussing the risk of permanent hair loss inside the company since at least 2006, but they never even included 'cases of permanent alopecia have been reported with' in the United States Taxotere label until 2015. The point being that Elizabeth Kahn was not warned and so could not give an informed consent to use Taxotere, because Sanofi never informed her. She was never given the choice, and was never told that there was another, equally effective option—Taxol—that didn't carry the same risk. She could have chosen that one or at least had the discussion with her oncologist; it should have been her decision to take the risk.

Why are oncologists so afraid to inform their patients of this risk? They cannot offer a warning if Sanofi doesn't inform them first. So why was Sanofi so unwilling to warn women and their doctors about the risk of permanent hair loss? We all know why, don't we? As the song says, 'money, money, money'. There was only one other taxane, the first taxane discovered: Taxol. And it is manufactured by Bristol-Myers Squibb.

On the bench next to me sat Jason Steinhart, associate vice president and associate general counsel, litigation at Sanofi (it was easy to find him on LinkedIn). I didn't particularly want to be sitting next to him, but I was damned if I was going to move. I'm sure he wasn't too keen about sitting next to me either, but more than likely he couldn't care less.

As Elizabeth was now getting a grilling, each answer she gave caused Mr Steinhart to snort, mocking it. Another reply from Elizabeth and another belittling scoff. I turned and gave him the look-of-death stare. *Can't he just shut his sneering mouth*? I was livid. He had the audacity to mock the witness AGAIN. I turned my head to stare at him again, letting out a loud tut and sigh. He returned my stare and moved away. The end of that day's session couldn't come quickly enough. It was uncomfortable, and I don't mean the bench or the air conditioning.

Desperate to get out, I couldn't face returning to the hotel yet. I needed to clear my jet-lagged brain and calm down. As I escaped the courthouse and said goodnight to the security men, I made my way down to the Mississippi River. I walked along its bank for an hour, passing the famous Café Du Monde, stopping to take photos of Jackson Square and the Washington Artillery Park. The light was quickly starting to fade, so I headed inland and located the famed Bourbon Street.

Before I knew it, I found myself walking into a little jazz bar in desperate need of a beer straight from the fridge and a trip to the toilet. While sitting on another hard wooden bench enjoying the cold amber nectar, I tried to pinpoint where I was on the map and couldn't believe how far away from the hotel I was. The long walk back was filled with memorable sights of packed bars with live music and fascinating art, vintage and voodoo shops. Music bursting out of every open door and buskers in the street added to the infectious vibe.

Eventually I made it back into my hotel's reception and was happy to see the food was still available. After a quick bite, I headed upstairs and into the shower. My thoughts soon turned back to Elizabeth, and I wondered how she would be feeling right then; how could she sleep that night?

CHAPTER THIRTEEN
You're Fired

Wednesday morning's courthouse entry started with security not bothering to check my ID or COVID-19 pass. I suppose I was easy to remember with my uncovered, shiny head and French paperwork. The usual security man asked me if I was a juror or a lawyer. The place seemed unusually quiet, and nobody else was there apart from me. This was weird. My jet lag felt like it was getting worse, and the brain fog was almost impossible to shake off.

Upon reaching the courtroom, I knew there was something strange going on. Five minutes before that morning's session and there was nobody around. A peek through the courtroom's glass panels showed two people attending to paperwork. Instead of pulling open the heavy wooden doors, I continued down the empty corridor to the history boards and looked out of the window, down to the street below. It was darker than normal. *If I don't go into the courtroom, I won't find out.* I did go in, and I did find out. It was 7:30 a.m., one hour too early. You know when you feel a fool? This was very much one of those times. I got very odd looks from the couple of staff already in the courtroom. There was no way I could sit down on a bench for an hour before court even started, so when the staff had their backs to me, I exited stealthily, hoping they would forget they'd seen me so I could go back to the corridor and spend an hour reading the local history boards.

All rise—eventually.

That day's session, with me sitting back on the chilly side, started with a drama before the jury even entered. Of course, why not? The judge had dismissed one of the jurors for being fast asleep during a lot of the evidence. I thought I knew which juror she was talking about as the one I had in mind had looked like he was sleeping most of the time. We were now down to seven jurors.

A couple of lawyers from each side addressed the judge from the lectern to put forward their objections to various things. I was straining to hear what they were saying. It wasn't easy, but then my ears pricked up when InTouch Solutions was mentioned. A lawyer for the plaintiff seemed to be objecting to the fact that Sanofi was being allowed to put to the jury that Elizabeth hadn't bothered to look on the internet to seek reasons as to why her hair wasn't growing back. Yet they, the plaintiff's lawyers, weren't allowed by the judge to mention the lengths Sanofi had gone to, trying to keep the information off the internet, hiring InTouch Solutions for that express purpose. How this could be fair and balanced was beyond me. It seemed very one-sided, in Sanofi's favour.

The jury was eventually called in.

All rise.

In walked the juror I thought had received his marching orders. In fact, the dismissed juror was the one sitting closest to the judge and not, as I'd thought, the one at the other end, closest to me. I couldn't help but wonder why the judge hadn't poked him with a big stick or had a private word with him during a break instead of leaving it till two days before the trial was due to finish. A couple of espressos during the day might have worked. What a start to the morning. All this time, Elizabeth had to wait patiently to be called up to begin being grilled again.

Elizabeth spoke about having to produce eight hundred photos for Sanofi. Of course, they went through them with a fine-tooth comb, looking for ones that contained the biggest smile or where she had her head tilted so the light would make it look like she had more hair than she actually had. We were all in the courtroom and could see her lack of hair. They were trying to show the jury that in fact her hair had fully grown back after her chemotherapy had finished but then she lost it again due to the natural aging process. This was such an insult, not to mention an outright lie. Insane. How were they allowed to do this? I wanted to scream. It was so unjust.

The jury looked interested in looking at the photos. This was NOT a good sign. They were making a meal of all the holiday snaps, her smiling and living a full, happy life. Thankfully, Elizabeth managed to say that we all smile for photos and that means nothing; it didn't portray how she felt inside. I could sense the irritation of the defence lawyer with Elizabeth's long, repeated answers and the fact that no matter how hard she tried, she couldn't break her.

At this point, with so much more to get through still, it didn't look like the trial was going to end the following day, but what did I know? My flight was booked for Friday afternoon, and I had to be there for the verdict. Eventually they had finished with Elizabeth. Phew!

Next up was Dr Glaspy, a haematology oncologist and a witness for the defendant. He started talking about labelling, TAX316, micrometastasis, and 'what is cancer?' He'd seen early-stage breast cancer patients treated with chemotherapy having increased survival rates instead of the old days of mastectomies. He discussed taxanes, adjuvant and neoadjuvant treatment, and how it takes one yew tree to produce a tiny amount of Taxotere. He was interesting, and the jury was paying attention. My stomach gurgled; it needed feeding.

Lunchtime.

When I reached security to leave the courthouse, I asked one of the officers what I would find if I took a right turn when I left the building, as I hadn't ventured in that direction yet. He said I'd come to the Waterside Shopping Mall in the Spanish Plaza, and he promised me it would only take ten minutes to get there. Off I marched. I would hate to be late back or not get a front row seat. Nobody puts baby in the corner or the back row!

The entrance to the mall from the bottom end of Poydras Street happened to be the furthest away from the food court. Following the directions, I eventually reached the far end and walked past the different counters, all with big queues. I spotted there was only a tiny line of hungry diners waiting to be served at the Chinese stall, so I picked the black peppered chicken Cantonese style and sat outside to eat, just a couple of metres away from the Mississippi River. It was so lovely to enjoy the view while eating delicious Chinese food, and for a fleeting moment, I thought about staying there for an hour or two.

Entering the courtroom after lunch, I decided on a change of scenery for the afternoon so took a seat on the front row of the Sanofi side. I don't even know if there are 'sides' as such, but that was how it seemed to me. Moments after I took my seat, Mr Jason Steinhart sat next to me.

All rise.

Dr Glaspy was back on the stand, talking about Elizabeth's diagnosis, treatment, and prognosis. The lawyer asked him if, from looking at the photos, he thought her hair had thinned. Mr Miceli, for the plaintiff, objected, and a sidebar followed for us to watch while listening again to the stirring voice of Louis Armstrong. Dr Glaspy was allowed to answer and said, 'Yes.' Looking at the jury, I got the impression they liked him and thought he was a credible witness. My heart started to sink. It's funny how suddenly, when you're least expecting it, the examination of a witness ends abruptly. This did. It was the plaintiff's counsel's turn, and Mr Miceli stood up.

He went straight for the jugular.

'You're not a dermatologist? You don't perform scalp biopsies?' This was obviously a rebuttal for Dr Glaspy being allowed to give his opinion about whether Elizabeth's hair had thinned over the years. I rearranged my butt on the bench. Suddenly the atmosphere was electric. Mr Miceli then asked Dr Glaspy if he informed his patients that hair loss could be permanent. My anger was immeasurable when he answered unapologetically, 'No.' I wanted to stand up and scream, 'What kind of human being are you?' After all the data and knowledge available, he still proudly refused to inform women. I was furious beyond belief.

This once composed, credible witness was now stuttering and seemed extremely uncomfortable under Mr Miceli's cross-examination. He was crumbling in front of our very eyes. It was amazing to observe. How easy the tables can be turned.

Dr Glaspy then had to admit that Taxotere and Taxol were equally as effective in treating early-stage breast cancer. Taxol doesn't carry the same risk of permanent hair loss that Taxotere does. This begs the question: why would an oncologist, knowing about the problem with permanent hair loss, give a patient the drug that can cause it instead of the drug that doesn't? What makes Sanofi's drug that much more appealing to him rather than Taxol, which Bristol-Myers Squibb makes?

Mr Miceli pressured him as to why he didn't inform patients about permanent hair loss. Under this fierce cross-examination, this witness was now probably doing more harm than good for the defence. And just when I thought it couldn't get any better, I overheard Mr Jason Steinhart turn to the woman sitting next to him and say, 'He's just destroyed us on this!' It was music to my ears and confirmed exactly what I was thinking; the only difference was that I was ecstatic about it, and he most definitely wasn't.

There then followed video evidence, depositions, and another sidebar. After came more questions about study TAX316 and yet another sidebar. If I didn't already know all the lyrics to 'What a Wonderful

World', I absolutely do now.

The cross-examination continued, and it seemed to me as if Mr Miceli were trying to connect Dr Glaspy to Sanofi to see why he seemed so biased towards them. There had to be a connection. Dr Glaspy was a principal in the organisation that performed Sanofi's TAX316 study. Sanofi paid Dr Glaspy to travel around the country to speak about using Taxotere. And when Sanofi needed an expert, well there was Dr Glaspy again.

The jurors created the impression of being interested in everything that day, but maybe they were unaware as to why the other juror was dismissed. Or it could have been because they knew the trial was drawing to a close, and it would soon be time to start their deliberations. I tried to picture them discussing everything they'd witnessed and wondered if it would be anything like the old black and white film *12 Angry Men*. Was it possible that one juror could change the minds of the others? Would we need a Henry Fonda fighting our corner?

This witness's nightmare cross-examination was finally over. I was sure the defence felt relieved, not to mention Dr Glaspy. The day's session was finished. It had been exhausting.

As I stepped out of the courthouse, the humidity sucked the air from my lungs, but the heat was great. *Will the trial really be over tomorrow?* I didn't know if there were any more witnesses. You see on TV how the jury can be out for days. My plane ticket was unchangeable. *Please let the verdict be in before my flight.* One less thing to think about was that as I was fully vaccinated against Covid-19, I didn't need to go searching for somewhere to get a PCR test to get back into France.

I paid the Waterside Shopping Mall another visit to buy the obligatory fridge magnets and got dragged into a beauty shop where a nice salesgirl treated me to a mini facial followed by a hard sell of their products that were going to eradicate my wrinkles. All the flying, jet lag, hot and freezing air plus wearing a facemask was playing havoc with my skin, so I and my skin very much appreciated this free facial treatment.

I spent the next two hours wandering around all the fascinating little streets of the French Quarter, lapping up the ambience. I passed groups of people waiting for their tour guides, and I cheekily sidled up to one gathering which was enjoying an animated 'ghost' tour. It would have been great to go on the trip that included a visit to the house used in the series *American Horror Stories: Coven*. I vowed to return one day.

It was a calf-aching trek back to the hotel as I had lost my bearings—a normal occurrence for me—but as darkness would fall as soon as I left the courthouse each day, it was a guarantee.

Happily collapsing into my spacious, snug bed, I burrowed under the quilt like a squirrel going into hibernation. I felt fragile, scared, and alone, and it wasn't even my trial. My thoughts turned to the lawyers who were working so hard for the women in these lawsuits, which was up to fourteen thousand women last time I'd checked. How would they be feeling? I was sure they wouldn't be getting much, if any, sleep that night, or did they take it all in their stride? By this time next day, it could be all over, and the years of challenging work for this trial would be over in a second. How were Elizabeth and her husband holding up? I shuddered to think about how the trial was going to end.

My mind wandered to the case of Amadou Diallo who, in 1999 while unarmed and in his own doorway, was shot forty-one times by four plain-clothes police officers. You wouldn't imagine there could be a remote possibility of those police officers being cleared after firing that many times at him. Wrong.

Some things seem so simple and clear-cut. Yet anything could happen in New Orleans for Elizabeth Kahn, especially as Sanofi appears to be a law unto itself, or acts as if it is, so nothing could be taken for granted.

CHAPTER FOURTEEN
It's a Wrap

A rumble of distant thunder and torrential rain stirred me from a restless sleep. *Where am I?* It took a while for me to realise it was my phone alarm that had disturbed me. All week I'd woken up an hour or two before the alarm went off, so today's sleep-in was a shock to the system. Lying there for a minute before unwrapping my cocooned arm to find my phone on the bedside table, I wondered if the thunder was an omen. It was a struggle to haul myself out of bed and into the shower.

I guessed the courtroom would be busy for the final day, so I made sure I got there a little earlier than usual, but not quite as early as the previous day when I'd made a mistake with the time, and took my place on the front bench of the plaintiff's side. Within minutes, the benches were full, full of suits. The atmosphere was fully charged.

All rise.

The judge entered and explained there had been a car incident involving one of the jurors. Oh my God! You couldn't make this up. Thankfully, they weren't injured, but they had to wait for the police to come and had no idea when that would be. I was sure the judge said that the police were aware it was a juror who was due in court, but whether that would make any difference or not we had no idea. It was decided that they would deal with motions and issues that could be managed without a jury present. About an hour and a half went by before the juror turned up.

All rise.

Defence counsel explained there was going to be video evidence—the deposition of Elizabeth's second oncologist, Dr Zoe Larned. In the video, the defence lawyers discussed Elizabeth's medical file, diagnosis, and treatment. Her demeanour was relaxed. I glanced at the jury who were all watching the big screen. Dr Larned was shown Elizabeth's blog, and they talked about PCIA, the role of chemotherapy, taxanes and what makes them different to other chemotherapy drugs, nurses' notes, dosages, risks, and warnings. It was obvious that Dr Larned liked Elizabeth very much, which was touching. The jurors were still engaged.

The video deposition continued. It was time for the cross-examination from Mr Darin Schanker, Ms Kahn's lead trial lawyer. They discussed alopecia, the distinct types and causes, the fact that Dr Larned did not qualify to offer expert opinion about Elizabeth's hair loss, and the fact that when she took over from Elizabeth's first oncologist, Dr Kardinal, he had already started Elizabeth on her Taxotere treatment. And Dr Kardinal had already testified that he was never told by Sanofi that Taxotere could cause permanent hair loss.

A great deal of time was spent going over all the health records Dr Larned created documenting each appointment with Elizabeth. On every one, Dr Larned had written 'hair is growing' NEVER 'grown', so this blew up the defence's lie that Elizabeth's hair had grown back fully and then dropped out again from age. This accusation from the defence was really something else and inexcusable. Dr Larned was a defence witness, so that was damning for them. It was a long deposition, but finally it ended.

That was it; all the evidence, all the witnesses, all done.

Now it was time for the closing arguments. My feeling of apprehension was overwhelming, and for the first time all week, I didn't notice the arctic blast. Everyone looked tense. This was it, folks, the endgame; all that work delivered and now resting on the wrap-up.

Darin Schanker stood up to go first. He refreshed the points: That Sanofi knew and hid permanent hair loss, and now Elizabeth Kahn had to live with it for the rest of her life. That Sanofi employees admitted the Taxotere label does not warn of PCIA. That Amy Freedman, Sanofi's former global safety officer, admitted Sanofi knew way back in 2006 that Taxotere could cause permanent hair loss. Yet this adverse side effect was not included on the informed consent form Elizabeth signed.

It was so engrossing that I didn't take any notes as I didn't want to miss a single thing.

It was then Sanofi's turn. Their lead defence lawyer, Hildy Sastre, stood up. She told the jurors she knew they were tired and wanted to go home and she understood that. In fact, she was so concerned about them, she reminded them how tired they were several times. She explained that Elizabeth was happy to sign the consent form which stated chemotherapy could cause serious side effects like blood clots and worse (death!) Yet the jury was supposed to believe that she wouldn't have signed it if it had stated the possibility of permanent hair loss. She then talked again about the jury being tired and how they must want to go home. *Really, is this even allowed*? I found her constant removal of her glasses only to put them back on seconds later, leaning and not leaning on the podium, really irritating.

She rounded up by telling the jury, 'I know you're tired and want to go home, so all you have to do is tick "no" to the first question, and you can all go.'

I'm no lawyer, but I found it hard to believe she could get away with telling the jury to do that when there were four questions they had to reach a unanimous decision on. Depending on how they answered the first question determined if they had to continue answering the other three. It was as if she was saying, 'Don't bother with any of the evidence; just tick "no" so you can go home.' The judge didn't seem to bat an eyelid, so it must be OK to do this.

The first question was:

Do you find by a preponderance of the evidence that Sanofi failed to take reasonable care to provide an adequate warning to Ms Kahn's prescribing physician of the risk of permanent chemotherapy-induced alopecia (PCIA) associated with Taxotere?

If the answer to question one is 'no', please sign the verdict form and return to the courtroom.

If the answer to question one is 'yes', please proceed to question two.

There were mutterings around me saying that Hildy Sastre had gone over her time by ten minutes. If true, how was this allowed?

Judge Milazzo then read out the jury charge instructing the jury what legal rules they should follow, which went on and on until the jurors were eventually allowed to leave the courtroom. I'm sure I wasn't the only one feeling sick. Now for the long wait. Well, hopefully a long wait as if it was a quick verdict, it probably wasn't going to be a verdict for the plaintiff.

Roughly ninety minutes later, the verdict was in.

We all filed back into the public gallery. The mood was sombre, and the facial expressions were those of unbearable angst on both sides.

It was a verdict for the defence.

If only the jury could have been told how Sanofi hired a Rapid Response Team to prevent it becoming common knowledge to breast cancer patients that Taxotere could result in permanent hair loss. If only the jury could have been told how Sanofi hired InTouch Solutions to try and silence me on social media. There were so many 'if onlys.'

I took my window seat on the first of my three flights home. So far it had been a day of goodbyes, which are never easy. As the plane's tyres left the runway, with my hands gripping the arm rests, my brain was a scrambled mess of thoughts. What an incredible trip this had been: sadness at the verdict, hope for the other trials in different US states, discovering a little of New Orleans. Being present at this trial had been an amazing experience, and I'd love to go to others in the future.

I felt as though I had renewed strength in my ability to carry on. Pushing from the back can be as important as leading from the front.

What now? Thousands of pending lawsuits will be heard across the different US states; this also means they will have different judges, and maybe some of them will allow crucial evidence to be heard. Who knows?

CHAPTER FIFTEEN
The Next Chapter

Where does that leave my story, my journey, and raising awareness? I was going to dare to say I'm sure that this trial is the end of it for me, but by now you all know how things go when I say this is the end.

I have ideas for the support group website, which was gifted to me by the owner, so I want to spend most of my time working on that, turning it into a non-profit association to give it credibility amongst other things, so I shall be on the hunt for sponsors and donors. Plus, I have my personal website and blogs to write. I certainly won't get bored. There is still so much to do. My work is far from done.

Since I finished the first draft of this memoir, there are a couple of exciting things that I have to tell you about.

The Fifth Circuit Court of Appeals overturned Sanofi's first trial win! This was FANTASTIC news with the retrial date set for the end of September 2022, but with things moving so fast, who knows?

I received an unbelievable invitation from Paxman Scalp Cooling, asking me if I'd like to host a session about PCIA for the world's first Scalp Cooling Summit they were organising. Would I? They told me to think about it, but really there was nothing to think about. The event was a massive success, and it filled me with hope that more and more oncologists are recognising how important a woman's hair is to her during chemotherapy. The benefit to a patient's mental health during treatment plays a big part not only in her life but that of her family too. It was an incredible experience, and I thoroughly enjoyed every minute. What an honour to have been invited to take part.

I believe I've managed to turn everything I've learnt over the last sixteen years into something positive that can help others. Hopefully I can continue to provide answers and to educate.

If any businesses reading this would like to buy a sponsorship package, please email me for details: admin@aheadofourtime.org.

One-off donations or anonymous donations can be made through the donate button:
www.aheadofourtime.org/copy-7-of-contact

I hope you've enjoyed this book and my story. I would so appreciate it if you do have a few minutes to leave a review on Amazon; it helps in many ways. Thank you so much for reading till the end.

MESSAGE FROM THE AUTHOR

If you'd like to get in touch with me or follow me on social media, you can do so via the following:

Facebook: www.facebook.com/SALedlie
Twitter: www.twitter.com/ShirleyALedlie
Website: www.saledlie.com
Instagram: www.instagram.com/shirleyledlie4549writer
Taxotears support group website: www.aheadofourtime.org
Support group email: admin@aheadofourtime.org
Personal email: shirleyledlie@zoho.eu

If you enjoyed reading *A Hair's Whisper*, you might like to check out my other memoirs which are all available on Amazon:

Naked in the Wind: Chemo, Hair Loss and Deceit
Mischief in Manhattan: Five Days in New York City
The Unexpected Pilgrim: Four Days in Israel
Ocean of Stars: My Vacation on Star Trek Cruise III

If you enjoy reading memoirs, I recommend you pop

over to the Facebook group We Love Memoirs to chat with me and other authors:

www.facebook.com/groups/welovememoirs

ACKNOWLEDGEMENTS

Some true stories just *have* to be told. This is one of them and not because it's my story but to bring attention to the fact there are many good people out there willing to help others and do the right thing.

First, I want to thank my husband, John, for encouraging me to write and for putting up with my chaotic writing process. I know how crazy it makes you.

David Miceli, I can never thank you enough for that incredible foreword; you have no idea how much it means to me. Your passion for your work has encouraged me to keep going and believe in myself. I have so much respect for you. Thanks for being my friend.

To my editor and proofreader, you know how much I appreciate all your help, but I wanted to say it again. Thank you so much, my friend.

Lynda, my writing buddy and friend, I would never get anything completed without your encouragement. Plus, our brainstorming coffees are such fun. Thank you.

Without the next group of people, there would be no *A Hair's Whisper: From Cancer to the Courtroom*. Actually, this has been probably the hardest part of this book to write.

Over the last five years, I've had the honour of

meeting and getting to know some of the lawyers willing to fight for the little people. Without you, there would be no litigation, no justice, and the cries from thousands of disfigured women would have gone unheard. You dared to take on one of the world's largest pharmaceutical companies when nobody else would. And I have absolutely no doubt you will be victorious. *Qapla'*, as the Klingons would say! David Miceli, Karen Barth Menzies, Ben Gordon, Dan Markoff, Zachery Wool, Chris Coffin, Lauren Davis, Mark Niemeyer, Darin Schanker, all the paralegals and backroom staff. I've formed friendships with some of you; those friendships are treasured.

Stella Reynolds and her extremely talented daughter Teddy Reynolds Hunt, LLB, LLM Inner Temple Bar student, I can't thank you both enough. Stella, we need a lunch date soon, and it's on me.

A big thank you goes to Ivan.

I want to give a huge shout-out for the *Ring of Fire* radio show. When I first came across *that* powerful video interview with Mr Papantonio and Mr Gordon, I knew the litigation would kick off. I've lost count of the number of times I've watched it.

A special thanks to the Paxman Scalp Cooling company. Your work is amazing and is already changing the face of cancer. After your own family experience, your devotion, expertise, and foresight will help millions of women worldwide not only to keep their hair while undergoing chemotherapy but help, if not totally prevent, PCIA. The world's first Scalp Cooling Summit you produced was ground-breaking, and I hope it won't be the last.

Denise Stevenson. Thank you for encouraging me

in my endeavours. You are doing wonderful things with www.double-zero.org

Last, but definitely not least, my cover designer. I love it. Thank you for seeing my vision.

Printed in Great Britain
by Amazon